GET OUT OF MY LIFE

Tony Wolf, Ph.D., is a practising clinical psychologist who has worked with children and adolescents for thirty years. He lectures frequently on parenting topics. He lives in Suffield, Connecticut.

Suzanne Franks was a BBC TV producer for many years and is now an academic, author and journalist. She has written *Dished! The Rise and Fall of BSB* (with Peter Chippendale) and *Having None of It: Women, Men and the Future of Work*. She has a teenage son and daughter (plus a formerly teenage daughter) and lives in London.

GET OUT OF MY LIFE – BUT FIRST TAKE ME AND ALEX INTO TOWN

Tony Wolf and Suzanne Franks

P

PROFILE BOOKS

This second edition published in 2008

First published in 2002 by
Profile Books Ltd
3A Exmouth House
Pine Street
Exmouth Market
London EC1R 0JH
www.profilebooks.com

10 9 8 7 6 5 4 3

Typeset in Bembo by
MacGuru Ltd
info@macguru.org.uk
Printed in the UK by CPI Bookmarque, Croydon, CR0 4TD

A CIP catalogue record for this book is available from the British Library.

ISBN 978 1 84668 087 8

Mixed Sources
Product group from well-managed
forests and other controlled sources
www.fsc.org Cert no. TT-COC-002227
© 1996 Forest Stewardship Council
FSC

Contents

Preface

This is a guide to adolescents – how to understand them, cope with them, and, to the extent that we can, direct their turbulent lives.

Teenagers of today have grown up in an era of far more lenient parenting practices compared with any previous generation. Their world may be complicated and scary; nonetheless, they feel more empowered than teenagers did in the past. They are more assertive and less directly obedient, especially at home. This change in teenage behaviour is real. It requires a similar change in teenage parenting.

This book differs from other parenting books in at least one crucial way. It does not offer a set of teenage parenting rules, though it does provide concrete sugges-tions on how to deal with a wide range of teenage issues. It explains why teenagers do what they do; it gives you the ability to translate teenage behaviour into its true, often less complicated meaning. Armed with this new way of seeing, parents will not need to be told what to do. They can make their own decisions, based on their general good sense and individual child-rearing beliefs.

An example:

'Louise, please could you lay the table?'
'Why are you always picking on me?'

If you understand the development issues embodied in this typical response, you can translate Louise's words:

No, I'd rather not lay the table. I would prefer to have
an argument with you.

Knowing the teenager's underlying message, parents can then respond as they wish. One option would be:

Don't you dare talk to me like that.

However, despite the intended lesson of the parent's words, namely that they really do not want to tolerate this kind of disrespect (which is a perfectly reasonable message) – their teenagers unfortunately will always interpret their response differently. They will hear:

Yes, I will fight with you.

And that leads them to respond:

I'll talk to you any way I want.

Which, translated, means:

Good, now let's keep this fight going, and with any luck you'll forget about laying the table altogether.

Parents with a clearer understanding of their teenagers' behaviour may choose alternatives to such a self-defeating response.

Throughout this book you will hear the re-created voices of teenagers and their parents. The quotes and conversations in the text are not from real people but a distillation of what really goes on. This will give you access to the real but never recorded discussions that take place in people's kitchens, in their heads, mumbled as they leave rooms, or screamed out in shopping centres. Their accuracy will be for you to judge. But many of you will recognise, as recorded nowhere else, those scenes that are a part of your life with a teenager. If you do, you will, we hope, be reassured. You are not doing anything wrong: everyone confronts the same kinds of problems with teenagers.

Living under the same roof as a teenager is frequently exasperating and painful. But at times they can also be entertaining and original as well as keeping us on our toes – providing us with an insight into everything from computers and mobile phones to contemporary culture. Much of what goes on between teenagers and their parents is often rather funny, if we can only step back far enough from our lives to view our daily travails for what they are, instead of as deadly serious issues.

Finally, if this book achieves its goal, you may notice a strange transformation in those scenes that used to drag you down. With a new understanding of your teenager's psychological development and state of mind, you may find that those scenes are never quite the same again. They look different, less desperate, more like the inevitable interaction between a normally developing teenager and a caring parent. You may also discover that, seeing things differently, you act differently as well.

Note to New Edition

This book was first published in the UK six years ago. In those few years much has changed in the world of adolescence, and this new edition has been updated with revised material on drugs, drinking and sex. There is also a new chapter about the ever-increasing influence of the electronic media and in particular the Internet. The basic issues of what goes on at home between parent and child, which is the book's main focus, are still of course the same. But what has changed and continues to change rapidly is the teenagers' world and the world into which they will grow up. This new edition contains an expanded section about the role of parents with their teenagers in a more uncertain world.

We used to think that the end of the Cold War would mean an era of greater peace and stability. Far from it. The early years of the new millennium seem far scarier and more unpredictable than the world was twenty years ago. The teenagers' world itself is also different: it seems ever faster, less clearly anchored. They will confront a future where you no longer simply grow up, get a job, bring up a family and grow old. Now you leave school or university and then see what happens; indeed this phase may last several years, often well beyond the end of higher education. Twenty-five is the new twenty-one. Adolescence is not only starting sooner, it is also continuing for longer than ever before. People are marrying – if at all – and having children at a much older age than was the norm only a few years ago. Teenagers today need a greater tolerance for uncertainty; they need to be more flexible, more prepared to accommodate change than in the past. As a result, family – those whom you can really rely on – becomes even more important.

Introduction

'Emily, please would you mind taking those dirty
glasses into the kitchen?'
'Why? They're not mine.'
'I don't care if they're not yours, Emily. You live in
this house and I am asking you to take those glasses
out into the kitchen.'
'But they're not mine. Why should I do it?'
'Emily, you're asking for it.'
'You're asking for it.'

Forty years ago the above conversation would rarely
have taken place, but it's common enough today.
Teenagers have changed. This is not an illusion.
Teenagers treat the adults in their lives in a manner that
is less automatically obedient, much more fearless, and

definitely more outspoken than that of previous generations.

> *'I would never have dared talk to my parents the way
> that Melissa does to me. Never.'*
> *'What would have happened if you did?'*
> *'I would have had a slap across the face.'*

True enough, but the harsher ways of dealing with children, especially physical punishment, are no longer viewed as acceptable, or in some cases even legal. Many parents still treat their children harshly; many still hit them. But such punishment is far less acceptable than it once was, even to those who do it.

We live in an era of 'child-centred' and 'permissive' parenting. As a result, the most effective weapons have been taken out of a parent's arsenal. No more hard smacks across the face for disrespectful answering back or when rooms are not tidied on demand. It's inevitable that without these harsher forms of enforcement, children's behaviour has changed. This is just human nature. The new teenager feels freer to answer back and to do as he or she pleases, especially at home.

The entitled teenager
Teenagers of today possess a distinct sense of entitlement. They have their rights, which they are only too well aware of. 'My parents are supposed to take care of

me. And they're not allowed to hurt me. They're supposed to protect me. I suppose that I should act better
towards them than I do. But even if I act like a prat,
they're still supposed to love me. No matter what I do.'
This is good. We want them to feel this way. We have
empowered our children and they feel the power. Still,
we did not think they would be so ungracious about it.
Ours is a generation of uncertain parents. We witness
our children's less restrained behaviour, and we do not
understand and we do not know what to do. We would
not have behaved that way. In the face of their
teenagers' insolence, parents feel frustrated, upset, and,
above all, inadequate. 'What can I do? I shout at her. I
ground her. I take away privileges. But none of it seems
to change her attitude.'

Nor do the teenagers benefit from their parents' frus-
tration. They become victims of the classic adolescent
paradox. While they demand freedom, and fight to
attain it, they still need to feel their parents' strength.
Teenagers battle to dismantle their parents' authority,
but they can find themselves adrift if too successful.
Anxiety, depression, even suicide can arise with the
added stresses of adolescence. A frequently quoted sta-
tistic is the alarming growth in teenage suicide. The rate
of suicide – especially amongst young men in the UK –
has steadily risen over the past thirty years. There are on
average around two suicides a day amongst young
people in the UK and Ireland and according to the

Samaritans, three teenagers in the UK attempt to self-harm every hour. Unquestionably, the more that adolescents feel themselves to be truly on their own and without their parents' support, the more vulnerable they are.

Yet for the average as opposed to the seriously troubled teenager, things are not nearly as bad as they may seem. The new teenager is not impossible to deal with. Parents must learn to adjust and to rely on a different kind of strength from that which their own parents used.

The new parent

'I'll tell you what the problem is. Teenagers today don't have any respect for their parents.' This is true. Old-style respect is gone. We have entered a new era in child-rearing. Perhaps the old way was both easier and more straightforward, but it is gone. Nostalgia is acceptable, but that style of parenting also had flaws. It was based in part on establishing fear. Creating fear as an explicit child-raising practice has some bad consequences. It can breed anger and resentment. It can intimidate and cause the intimidated to lose confidence in themselves. Perhaps worst of all, it tells children that in the service of getting what one wants, fear and intimidation are necessary and acceptable in everyday life.

Teenagers today are not pliable, and they say what is on their mind – always. They live in a society which has seen an overall decline in deference to all kinds of authority, including parents. Yet for all their rudeness, especially at home, it is not clear at all that as adults these teenagers will be 'worse' than their parents, either less caring or less motivated. They may be more caring and more motivated. They may, in turn, be better parents.

Besides, it is possible to elicit respect from teenagers; it's just of a different kind than the old version. This new respect can only be based on the strength and confidence of parents. This kind of strength of character is not as easy to come by as a strength based on the cane or the belt. More confidence is required to employ this strength. With few apparent weapons in their arsenal, parents must stand up to all that their teenagers may dish out, and still come out with their heads high, their confidence intact, their position as the parents and the bosses still acknowledged, if grudgingly. It is not easy. But it is possible.

The first step is to accept a child's right to say what he or she has to say, no matter how stupid or unreasonable. You don't have to listen to all of it, you can leave whenever you want, but you respect their right to say it. Then you say what you have to say, you stand your ground and are not blown away by the inevitable response. This kind of parenting earns respect. It's the strength not to descend to teenagers' level of name-calling, when they would lose respect for you. It's the strength to walk away.

*'Don't you dare talk to me that way, Eleanor. When
are you going to show some proper respect? I don't
know what's wrong with you. You are going to have to
get your act together.'*

Eleanor rolls her eyes.

*'Don't you roll your eyes at me. Do you want a smack
on the face?'*
'Go ahead. Hit me. I dare you.'

Eleanor knows that the time for that was over with
years ago. Perhaps the greatest skill for a parent today is
learning not to be hurt, truly understanding that what
teenagers say and scream means nothing other than that
they are teenagers and this is how teenagers today
behave, understanding that what they say and what they
do in no way diminishes who you are and what you do.
Your teenage children cannot diminish you unless you
allow them to do so. 'That all sounds very simple. But
in the real world how can we as parents have the
strength to rise above the daily onslaught?' You need
confidence – not confidence that you are always
making the right decision (nobody can do that) or that
you are always in control of the child (nobody can even
come close to achieving that), but rather the confidence
that you are the right person for the job and that your
efforts are definitely not in vain.

You must understand what you say does have an impact on your teenager, despite much evidence to the contrary. You must know that you need not be perfect, that you can make mistakes.

You may not like what I am saying. You may disagree with my decisions. You may truly think that I am wrong. I may in fact be wrong. But I am your parent and the decisions that I make are in my judgement what I think is best. Whether you like it or not, you are stuck with me. That won't change, at least not for the next few years. And that is the way I want it.

There is a pleasant irony to all this. If parents can hang on through the teenage years, they may get all that they ever wanted at the end of the process: an adult child who genuinely likes and respects you and is at ease with you; a person genuinely considerate of others and, amazingly, considerate of you; a grown child who now appreciates all that you have done for him or her.

You were a wonderful parent, even though I know that I gave you such a hard time.

PART ONE

Adolescence

I

What is Adolescence?

*Alison was such a delightful child. She was always
drawing sweet little cards with hearts or smiley faces on
them. They would say 'I love you, Mummy.' She was
a treasure. She really was. I used to call her
'Mummy's little treasure'. And helpful around the
house? She would always ask if there was anything she
could do. I just don't understand what happened. She
changed. And now she abuses me. She's a monster.*

*Daniel and I always had a special relationship. We
were very close. When he got home from school, he
couldn't wait to tell me about his day, and he always
wanted to show me his work from school. He was so
proud of it. Sometimes he would sit in my lap, he
wasn't embarrassed about it, and we would just talk. It*

was really wonderful. But then he changed. Now he hates me. He can't stand to be near me. I can't touch him. I've lost him. I feel so awful, so rejected.

Adolescence is unlike any other period in life. Above all, it is a time of transformation. It is not a single event, but a number of major changes coming within a relatively short period. These changes turn nice little children into intimidating adolescents.

There are distinct differences between how boys and girls go through this traumatic period of their lives. Not all adolescent boys and girls behave in the ways described throughout this book, but there is no question that certain patterns of behaviour are characteristic of each sex. And there are very real reasons why these patterns exist.

When does the process start? There is no clear beginning. Girls generally mature earlier than boys, both physically and emotionally; and often they have most of the characteristics of adolescence by age twelve and a half, although there is some evidence that the average age of physical maturity – menstruation / breast development – is getting lower. Boys, on average, mature about a year later. But whenever the change begins, it will often seem rather sudden: one day a child, the next, something quite different.

With boys, the change may begin that first day when he subtly checks his appearance in the mirror before leaving the house. With girls, it seems to happen on an otherwise uneventful day – a day that occurs with inexplicable frequency sometime around the February of Year Seven. That's the day when Charlotte comes home from school and is asked to do something that in the past she has done quite willingly, even enthusiastically. But on this day – the first day of her adolescence – she turns to her parents and snaps, 'Why are you always on at me to do that? You've got hands, too, you know.'

Physical changes

What are the changes of adolescence? The most obvious ones are physical. The children get a lot bigger – not gradually, as they have been doing all along, but suddenly. Girls mature before boys, of course, so that a Year Eight class offers the humorous spectacle of huge women walking side by side with little kids.

The bodies don't simply grow. They change. Girls, for whom the changes are probably more significant, take on a whole new shape. Their hips widen and their breasts develop. Boys develop more muscle, grow hair in new places, and confront a very different-looking set of genitals. When this physical maturation is finished, boys and girls look at themselves and do not see the same person who was there not long before.

Adolescence is the start of true sexuality. Girls menstruate. Boys produce sperm. Most important of all, both sexes begin to have sexual feelings. Prior to adolescence, during the period referred to as 'latency', they had such feelings, but for the most part these were underground. Pre-teens do have some interest in sex and can engage in sexual activity, but it really is a low priority:

> 'Hey, wanna see my new PSP?
> 'Yeah. Go on, show me.'
> 'Hey, d'you wanna see a picture of a naked woman?'
> 'Yeah, sure. Is it okay if I look at her later?'

With the dawning of adolescence, the naked-lady pictures knock the PSP into oblivion. The sexual feelings brought on by the biological changes of adolescence are unavoidable. Like it or not, here we are! And these feelings change everything. Suddenly the world has a whole new appearance. Previously a neutral canvas, it is now imbued with sexuality. And the way in which the new adolescent experiences it is changed forever.

Intellectual changes

> 'Mum, Aunt Ellen and Uncle Ralph are probably
> going to get a divorce, aren't they?'
> 'Who told you that?'
> 'No one. I just can tell by the way you and Dad talk
> about them.'
> 'Dad, Mrs Williams is very insecure, isn't she?'

'What do you mean?'
'You know, the way she always acts so pretentiously.'

In addition to changes in sexuality, a less obvious but nonetheless very important change of adolescence is that thinking processes jump to a whole new level. Teenagers understand concepts and abstractions in a way they were not capable of before. They can participate in adult conversations (although they probably will rarely choose to). They can see the world through adult eyes (although they often refuse to). In short, the world of the adolescent is infinitely more complex than the one he or she had known before.

The major change: turning away from childhood

All kinds of changes, physical and intellectual, mark adolescence. But the hallmark of adolescence – the transformation that defines this period of life – is a psychological change. It is the adolescent mandate. A new and powerful voice rises from within the child. They must obey this voice and, in doing so, their lives change forever.

Simply put, the mandate tells the adolescent to turn away from childhood and childish feelings. Since childhood is marked by the domination by parents, it follows that adolescents must turn away from their parents.

Before adolescence children were ... children, and they were free to act and feel as children. They could love their parents openly and depend on them. But with adolescence, a new force within dictates that teenagers must now experience themselves as independent, and be able to exist on their own. No more can they feel close to or dependent upon their parents.

This mandate eliminates the wonderful security of childhood. Day-to-day living takes on a quality of desperation. The independent self of childhood, which had been content to develop a basic competence in such matters as tying shoes and riding a bicycle, but always with Mummy and Daddy as a safety net, now begins to assume for itself the full responsibility for survival. Life is no longer a game. It is for real. Yes, the world has become an exciting place, but in this new world adolescents feel much more exposed and therefore more vulnerable than ever before. Things can get scary, even terrifying, and perhaps overwhelming.

This turn towards independence, towards a world separate from family and home, has always been at the core of adolescence, today and a thousand years ago. It is an inevitable process. More than anything else, it is responsible for most of the behaviour that constitutes contemporary adolescence.

The wish not to grow up

The course of pre-adolescent childhood is played out in the continuing struggle between the drive to grow up and the wish not to. On the one hand there is the 'baby self' which desires only the nurturing it has enjoyed for years. All pleasure. No fuss. 'After a hard day at school let me unwind and fill up with good sensations. Let me watch television and eat crisps. I definitely do not want to hang up my coat.'

Parents see their children being immature, irresponsible, lazy and demanding, because the home is the natural realm for expressing the dependent, babyish mode of functioning.

But there is the other self beginning to develop slowly – the independent, mature self. This self reaches out and seeks gratification from meaningful interaction with the world. It sets forth to accomplish something, to develop competence. It is willing to deal with stress, to take on responsibility. It is even willing to hang up coats – but only at school, or at Grandmother's house. It is usually on view only away from the home, unseen by parents.

Normal development pushes towards an ever-decreasing role for the baby self. Adolescence is no more than the first, most traumatic stage in this ongoing struggle, exacerbated by the new awareness of sexuality and the mandate to separate from parents, to avoid unacceptable feelings of dependence. Once people reach adolescence and, ultimately, adulthood, most of them will have resolved this conflict by choosing a life of growth and separation. This 'decision' is what we label maturity. This is what's supposed to happen. Ultimately, young people can be pleasant even towards their parents. But not during adolescence! Then, they very much remain children when they are home. And often rather nasty children. This is a crucial point: operating in the baby-self mode is a way not to separate from the parents.

Some children seem able to move off to function independently more easily than others. Their trials of adolescence will be relatively smooth for all concerned. Other children, although unaware of their choice, remain far more eager to seek the bliss of unseparated babyhood and avoid the hassles of dealing effectively with the world around them. Some children need to cling, often provoking endless and senseless battles. Children who are not so good at functioning on their own will probably have a tougher adolescence than their peers.

Madeleine and the stairs
During childhood the two selves exist side by side, switching back and forth. When Madeleine was not yet 2 years old, she would sit at the bottom of the stairs and cry for twenty or thirty minutes. This happened almost every day for at least two months. That is a lot of crying.

Madeleine's bedroom was upstairs, and she had already learned to go up and down the stairs by herself. The crying was her means of announcing that she still wanted to be carried up to her room. Sometimes – when she felt like it – she would go up the stairs by herself. At those times she actually liked the climb. But, for whatever reason, Madeleine chose this issue on which to take a stand. And she devoted an enormous amount of time and energy to trying to make her parents carry her up the stairs.

Why? What was so important that day after day Madeleine would make such a scene, and stay with it for so long?

Madeleine was confronting a serious hurdle. During the first part of her life, once she began to interact with her world, she had been Queen of the Universe. What she wanted her parents to do, they did. Her will was their will. There was no separation. But then, to her delight but also to her horror, Madeleine discovered that this did not have to be the case.

She had already tried the 'no' experiment and discovered its results. A parent says, 'Come here', and a child says 'No'. The child then watches her own body to see whom it will obey. To her delight it always obeys her. But up until a child's first open defiance, she has no way of knowing who is in charge of her body because at first she believes that she is a continuum of her parents.

The experiment has a second part. That is what Madeleine was fighting for on the stairs. 'It's sort of all right that I'm in charge of me. But I certainly don't want to give up being in charge of you, Mummy and Daddy. If it is true that we are totally separate and have separate wills, then it means that I am actually on my own and that is not so good. For then I am alone and very little. I will have to do everything for myself. I will have to learn how to survive. And I do not like any of that. I prefer the old way.'

Madeleine was fighting to remain the absolute ruler of the universe – without any obligations or responsibilities. Who wouldn't?

The bliss of the baby self

The baby self does not die easily. In fact, it lives on somewhere in all of us. It desires not just to rule the world but also to move back in time to the absolute bliss of babyhood, wrapped in Mother's arms, forever.

It is the baby self which, above all, is responsible for most of the day-to-day problems that parents have with their children and teenagers. Although adolescents reject the child in themselves, it remains very much present in aspects of their behaviour. And although teenagers refuse to accept that they are in any way childish, they all act in a childish manner. The mandate of adolescence cannot dismiss the child. It only decrees that the baby self is no longer welcome. With their parents, adolescents have made their earliest and most powerful attachment. We continue to touch them in a way that no one else can because there is an underlying and long-standing deep bond of love. But since our connection with them is the strongest, it is the most difficult to break.

The alternation between these two distinctly different selves, one mature, one babylike, is not only bewildering to parents. See-sawing between these extremes can also drive us crazy. It's normal and healthy but it's not much fun to deal with.

A teenage version of 'Madeleine and the stairs' would be this scene between Vanessa and her mother:

'Mum, can I go shopping with Julie and Kate after tea?'

'No, dear, you know you're not allowed out on school nights.'

'But, Mum, please. I'll be home by eight. You know that's when the shopping centre closes.'

'No, Vanessa. We don't want you out during the week.'

'Mum, you're not being fair. You let Stephen do all kinds of stuff just because he's a boy.'

'Stephen is older and, besides, that has nothing to do with it. I said no and that's final.'

'I hate you. You never let me do anything. Why? Why can't I go?'

'Vanessa, you are starting to make me angry.'

'You're getting angry? I'm the one who's not allowed to go out. Why, Mum? You just like ruining my life.'

The confrontation continues. Vanessa ends up in tears and storms off to her room, where she sulks for the rest of the evening. Her mother also remains in a bad mood.

This was not the first time that there had been such a scene, nor would it be the last. From previous experience, Vanessa knew full well what her mother's response to her request would be. Not only that, she knew the scene would end exactly as it did. Parents who have endured such scenes remember distinctly feeling that their child was after something, something more than just getting them to change their mind. From Vanessa's mother's standpoint, Vanessa seemed to be after a smack in the face. If not that, then what did she want?

Why couldn't Vanessa accept 'No' as an answer, especially after a couple of attempts to change her mother's mind hadn't worked?

Vanessa was being asked to agree to something she did not like. And this meant shifting over, however briefly, to her more adult, independent mode of functioning. She might have decided: 'Well, it's really no big deal. I would like to have gone out. I would have had fun. But I see them every day at school. It's no big loss. Anyway I can call Julie and chat to her.' But picking up and moving on was not for Vanessa. On another day she might have accepted defeat – even gracefully. This time, especially because it was her mother – the object of her strongest, most babyish attachment – the baby inside her dictated the scene.

Separation, which would have ended the contact, was absolutely not what Vanessa wanted. Had she accepted the 'No' her involvement with her mother would have been brief, but she kept after her mother and a lengthy scene ensued. Instead of separation, Vanessa achieved just the opposite, just what she wanted. She got passionate involvement over an extended period of time, even if it was in the form of yelling, crying and sulking.

Not only can the baby within the teenager control their behaviour. It can achieve this without their knowledge. Teenagers have an infinite capacity for self-deception. 'Me acting childish? No. My Mum's the baby. She's the one who isn't mature enough to change her mind. I'm just trying to get to be a little more independent. She's the one who needs to grow up and get a life.'

This is actually how they think. Acting like a baby? Even when they are yelling at parents who have locked themselves in a bathroom to escape the harangue, they are certainly not behaving childishly. No way.

A self without conscience

This is a characteristic of the baby self. It does not look at itself. It does not judge itself. It is not bad. It is not good. It is not anything. It has no conscience. 'I'm not good-looking. I'm not ugly. I'm not a good person. I'm not a bad person. I'm not anything. When I'm home,

I'm just plain old me.' That's why adolescents can be so infuriatingly oblivious to their own behaviour.

> *'How can you act this way?'*
> *'What way?'*

They are not being intentionally difficult. In some kind of magical way, what they do at home exists in a sphere of its own. It has nothing to do with the adolescent's sense of self, with the kind of person he or she really is. They simply do not look at themselves. This is not something that the baby self does.

> *'Are you honest?'*
> *'Yes.'*
> *'But you just lied to your parents.'*
> *'Yes, I know. I know I lied, and I know it doesn't make sense, but I am honest. Lying to my parents or my brother or sister is just not the same thing as lying to somebody outside the family.'*
> *'You mean lying to your parents is not dishonest?'*
> *'Well, yes, it is, but I am not a dishonest person. I'm really not. I can't explain it. It just is that way.'*
> *'But you shouldn't lie to your parents, should you?'*
> *'No, I suppose not.'*
> *'You suppose not?'*
> *'I mean if it's bad, it's not very bad. It's just not the same as it is with everyone else.'*

Which is the real self?

Which is the real self, the impossible teenager who gives her parents nothing but grief and would seem to prefer death to helping around the house, or the quite amenable young person who assists her grandmother with household chores? The boy who will not take out the rubbish at home – a routine chore for the previous three years – even when he trips over it, or the one who receives a prize at school for his extraordinary efforts on 'Pick up your Litter' day? The girl who looks like a slob when at home, or the one who preens for over an hour to get ready to go out?

Both identities are normal and necessary. Yet if parents want to know what their children are really like, if they want to get a sense of who their children will become as adults, the more accurate gauge is behaviour away from home. The self that adolescents bring out to deal with the world is, in fact, a truer reflection of the real level of maturity they have achieved. At the very least, the behaviour that parents see and endure at home is not necessarily the behaviour their children exhibit elsewhere.

The passion of adolescence

Adolescence is unlike any other period in life. With it comes a special feeling, one that we never quite forget. During this time, attention and concern turn to the world outside, and away from family and home. Sexual feelings, newly emergent, increase the nature and intensity of that focus. The result is that the world becomes infused with incredible power and poignancy. The world is new – but this newness has a price.

As adolescents cut off dependence on home and parents, they feel much more on their own. And although not yet established in the big outside world, they can no longer use home as a fallback. Successes and failures in school and with friends seem absolutely crucial to continuing survival. Everything takes on a much more desperate quality. Because adolescents do not have much experience in life, they see only their day-to-day existence. They have no long-term perspective. None.

The world has become an exciting place, but in it they feel much more exposed, much more vulnerable than ever before. Moreover, their feelings have an undeniable power – a power that makes adolescence, however troubling, very, very special.

Where it's at

A typical memory of adolescence is listening to a song on the radio that you liked, but also feeling pressure to turn to another station just in case it was playing an even better song. No matter how good the first song there was always the danger of missing out on something even more special.

Teenagers wander up and down the same stretch of

road always on the lookout. They phone or text each other incessantly or hang out in the street near a coffee shop talking in small groups or just waiting for something to happen. There is an expectancy in the air so real they can almost reach out and touch it.

> *'Hey, Joel, anything happening?'*
> *'Naah. I just texted Sam and Josh and they said maybe there was going to be a party at some girl's house that I never heard of. I don't know. We'll probably hang about here, see if anything turns up. How about you?'*
> *'Dunno. It's been pretty dead around here, except there's this kid Rob who's supposed to be looking for Harry Bronson 'cause he's pissed off with him for something. But I don't know. We'll probably stay around here a while and then maybe go into town.'*
> *'Yeah, we might come in too.'*

Life is very powerful stuff for a teenager. It holds them continually in thrall. They cannot put the feeling into words, but they have a sense that something could happen out there that really would be what they're waiting for. It is both tantalizing and frustrating.

> *'What time is it?'*
> *'I don't know. I think it's about 10.30.'*
> *'I don't think anything's going to happen.'*

*'Yeah. I'm probably just going to go home. I'll give
you a call tomorrow.'*
'Yeah. See ya later.'

But adolescents would not want to go home until they were fairly sure that it was late enough. Late enough so that nothing would happen without them. They would not want to chance missing it. The arrival of mobile phones and the new possibilities they provide for communication between teenagers have further intensified these sensations.

What is the something that infuses the very air with unspoken potential? Sexuality, certainly, but it is more than that. Prior to adolescence, children have loved their parents, perhaps a favourite pet, or experienced other attachments that are part of home. But with adolescence this capacity for passionate involvement and love, though it does not totally leave home, turns outward. However, it has little to attach to, especially in early adolescence. It lacks focus.

Only from adolescence onward can humans fall in love. In early adolescence such love is usually limited to powerful but transient crushes. Only later are deeper, more lasting love relationships formed. Mostly an adolescent's love is unfocused, diffuse. It lights up the whole world and produces the sense of inchoate longing that so characterises early adolescence. Teenagers are, in effect, in love with the world, but their love is unrequited. They have great longings, but are never quite fulfilled.

Memories of adolescence

A song from our past, a particular place, even just a smell can suddenly evoke in all of us the sense of another time and place. With this casting back in time comes a surge of feeling, poignant but fleeting, gone before we can catch hold of it. We picture clearly a piece of our adolescence, and we experience a deep longing. Yet the scenes that cause these feelings are often oddly unremarkable.

We might recall summer evenings with a group of friends wandering in the park or congregating at a pavement café before going off to a party. The reality may not always have been so exciting. But the memories stir up that special adolescent feeling of being in love with the world. They recall a sensation of the unique, unfocused passion of adolescence.

2

What They Do
and Why

The two main forces of adolescence are the onset of sexuality and the mandate that demands that teenagers turn away from childhood and parents. More than anything, these two forces shape adolescence. But their shapes can be strange, and they are usually very different for boys and girls. Though the underlying adolescent forces are similar for both sexes, what they produce is quite different.

Most teenagers do not act at all as they did when they were younger. Above all, how they act often does not seem to make sense.

Facing the adolescent mandate –
allergy to parents

Alan was sitting on the sofa watching television. His mother sat down next to him.

What are you watching?

Without a word Alan got up and left, went to his room, and turned on his stereo.

Mother: *I'm not good enough for him? He's repelled by me?*
Alan: *I can't help it. I'll be perfectly relaxed, and as soon as she walks into the room, I feel all tense and uncomfortable. It's not her fault. I can't explain it. I just don't like being near her and the same goes for my Dad.*
Mother: *But it seems like he hates me. Do I disgust him or something? Why? What's the matter with him?*

It is the teenager's allergy to his parents. Even a parent's presence in the same room causes real discomfort. Worse yet, the parents might actually say, 'Hello', or 'How was school?' It is enough to make their teenager's skin crawl. They cannot wait to get away, cannot wait for their parents to shut up. Being near their parents creates feelings of wanting to be near them, as always before, feelings of loving them and wanting their love.

But these feelings are now totally repugnant. And because parents are the source of these unacceptable feelings, adolescents are repelled by their own parents. They still have feelings that pull them towards their parents, but these feelings are also completely unacceptable to them.

'Just occasionally I would like him to sit in the room with me for a full five minutes so we can talk about our day. I do not think this is an unreasonable request.' It is not. Parents are allowed to order their sons to stay in the room with them, even order them to talk. But the sons will squirm. Girls, of course, will not only squirm but also take intentional deep breaths, tap their feet and roll their eyes or fiddle with their phone.

Teenagers do not like to be touched by their parents for the same reasons that they do not like to be near their parents. It is still okay to give them hugs and kisses, but understand that they will squirm and try to get away.

The patterns of behaviour caused by this allergy differ markedly for boys and girls. Boys, primarily because of their sexuality, choose the absenting method in dealing with Mum and Dad. They hide. Girls battle. Not all boys hide and not all girls fight, and not to the same degree, but there's no question that certain patterns of behaviour are characteristic of each of the sexes.

Teenage boys
Vanishing experts

Once adolescence begins, teenage boys go to their room, close the door, turn on their stereo, and come out four years later. This scenario is not that much of an exaggeration. Some also spend a lot of time away from the house – a solution available to them because teenage boys are usually given more freedom than girls. In short, boys solve the problem of their need to separate from their parents by doing just that: physically separating. They become vanishing experts. They learn the trick of saying 'yes' but doing 'no'. They agree to do what is asked of them, in order to avoid a fight, but then disappear before actually accomplishing the task in question.

> *'James, could you empty the dishwasher?'*
> *'Sure, Dad, in a minute.'*

And then James is gone.

Above all, teenage boys become very private. They do not like to talk to their parents. In fact, they do not want their parents to know anything about what is going on in their life. The main reason is their sexuality. These feelings are an enormous part of a teenage boy's world. And this sexuality is something that he very much wants to keep separate from his parents. But it is also so much a part of him that the only way to keep it separate from them is to keep himself separate. The internal taboo against mixing sex and parents is so strong, and the role of sexuality in a teenage boy's life is so pervasive, that he is forced for the most part to shut his parents out of his life. And once again new technology, in particular the ubiquitous mobile phone, has increased this scope for teenage privacy. No one need ever call their house or leave messages there and teenagers no longer need to have phone conversations with their friends within earshot of the family. So parents are even less likely to know what is going on.

The problem of Mummy

Boys are especially likely to avoid their mothers. Most adolescent boys are attracted to women. For most boys there has already been one particular woman in their life whom they have loved deeply. Unfortunately, that woman is their mother. Hence, until they get their new and fairly amorphous sexuality firmly focused on females outside the home, their mother presents a problem. The possibility always exists that strong feelings in connection with a boy's mother might be tinged with sexuality and might therefore become really unacceptable. In fact, because everything with adolescent boys is so sexualised, strong feelings towards anybody are a problem until that sexuality is better focused.

Particularly troubling from the perspective of the mother is that her previously open, talkative, very huggable boy disappears absolutely and is replaced by a young man who seems to radiate an aloofness that, if anything, makes her feel scorned. The situation can create real problems. Hurt by her son's aloofness and feeling rejected, a mother may aggressively communicate her hurt to her son, which is the worst thing she can do.

> *'Why? Why do you act this way? You hate me, don't you? You actually hate me.'*
> *'Jesus Christ, Mum, will you leave me alone. You don't know anything.'*
> *'There. You're doing it. You hate me.'*
> *'For Christ's sake, Mum. Will you shut up!'*
> *'Why? Why are you behaving like this?'*

Since strong emotional contact with his mother is especially upsetting to any teenage boy, he may in turn react strongly to his mother's anger at him. After all, he can't explain the facts of life to his mother because he doesn't really know what's going on himself. Can we imagine the following speech? 'It's not anything to do with you, Mum. It's my strong instinctive but normal reaction against my sexually tinged dependency needs. It won't be nearly as bad in a few years when I am more truly independent and when my sexuality is better focused on women outside the home.' No, we can't imagine or expect this insight.

There is no solution for a mother beyond understanding that at this point in her son's life, he needs distance from her. She must accept his behaviour, understand that its root is not dislike for her, and realise that in time it will change – and it will – when he becomes more truly independent – when he has his own sexuality better under control.

Fathers and sons

What about fathers and sons? Fathers, too, are to be avoided, but the ban is not so stringent. The sexual taboo is not such a major distancing factor, but closeness and affection have to be carefully censored in order to avoid any sense of homosexuality. When fathers and sons are able to maintain contact it's usually in some sort of oblique relationship. They do not exactly relate to each other, but they can discuss topics of mutual interest, typically football, thereby at least keeping open a line of communication.

> 'Dad, did you see that amazing Michael Owen goal last night?'
> 'I know, ever since he's come back from injury Newcastle have been brilliant.'
> 'I just hope he's okay for the England match next week.'

But many boys cannot even tolerate that level of interaction.

Fight or flight

Boys for the most part cannot battle verbally. They get little practice. They may engage in unsophisticated verbal sparring with their peers ('Stop being such a knob'; 'You're such an arsehole') but past a certain point, the prevailing code says that you have to fight. Boys rarely develop the skills or the emotional capacity to stay with strong verbal scenes. The typical adolescent boy history includes few direct child–parent screaming matches.

If boys do become emotional with their parents, they tend to get very emotional indeed. These occasional instances are often accompanied by a punched hole in the wall or shattered glass panes when a door is slammed too violently as the boy storms out of the house. Boys avoid confrontation for the excellent reason that they can't handle it. They get too upset. It's either fight or flight, and at home they usually do the latter – which is just as well.

Boys who do battle regularly with their parents instead of isolating themselves can create serious problems. They are usually boys who, prior to their teenage years, remained strongly attached to their parents. In adolescence, their lack of separation takes the form of endless battling. With the addition of sexuality to their already strong feelings, the emotional scenes that such a boy provokes can become overwhelming for him. Serious – even scary – problems can result, and we will refer to these later on. Fortunately, it is more normal for teenage boys to have as little to do with their parents as they can.

Couch potatoes

One particularly irritating manifestation of this mandate in boys is a sort of absenting even when present. What happens is that teenage boys – as so brilliantly immortalised in the Harry Enfield character 'Kevin' – develop terminal lethargy. They seem to catch a lengthy case of sleeping sickness. They appear to do nothing. If the normal speed of human activity is thirty-three or forty-five rpms, teenage boys seem to go at around six. Words like 'wha?' and 'huurh?' enter their vocabulary.

> *'Michael, would you help me move the garden chairs into the garage?'*
> *'Wha?'*

> *'Alexander, are these your empty coke cans in the lounge?'*
> *'Huurh?'*

These boys have their new sexuality and they also have their future, which hangs like a disquieting cloud, ever threatening. 'Do you really think you can make it on your own?' Boys do not like such thoughts. Such thoughts are disturbing. At home boys want peace and tranquillity. In this regard parents are a special problem because they are a constant potential source of aggravation.

Didn't you say you had a history test tomorrow? Shouldn't you be doing some work?

Boys seek to achieve a state of perfect passive pleasure. So do girls, but boys seem to do it more. Teenage boys seem to be particularly good at lying in bed, listening to music, watching TV and doing nothing. They can get themselves into a state of total passivity, with no anxiety and with genuine comfort, screening out all unpleasant stimuli. But it must be worked at. The teenage boy's pledge of behaviour is something like the following: 'I will do what I feel like doing, but, just as important, I will not do what I do not feel like doing. I will do my best to deal with my adolescence by devoting my life at home to feeling as good as possible at all times. And, above all, I am going to avoid anything that is not going to make me feel good.'

They may never achieve it but they try.

Do you know what Mark did during the Easter holidays? He did nothing. You don't understand. I mean absolutely nothing at all.

Teenage girls
The never-ending battle

Girls will in most cases deal with the psychological dilemma of adolescence differently from boys. Like boys, adolescent girls find it totally unacceptable to feel attached to, or dependent on, their parents. But girls do not withdraw. Unlike boys, they do not have to. Instead they fight. It is with girls, not boys, that parents experience the supreme disruption of adolescence. Charming, co-operative daughters turn, often rather suddenly, into hysterical, shrieking monsters.

Girls solve the problem of living at home, and yet successfully combating their totally unacceptable feelings of love and dependence, by fighting everything. 'Whatever my parents say, I will shriek at, do the opposite of, disagree with. You say it, I'll yell at it. By doing this, I am obviously demonstrating, both to myself and to you, that I am not dependent and loving. How can I be anything other than independent of my parents if everything that they say to me I scream at? Also, whenever I think I can get away with it, I will cheat and lie.'

Sylvia actually told me that she wished that I had put her in a foster home when she was a baby, rather than grow up with me as her mother.

My Jennifer swears at me all the time.

41

Lydia told me to shut up. Can you imagine, just like that, she said to me, 'Shut up!'

The major reason that teenage girls stay involved with their parents – however combatively – is that their new sexuality does not work against them. Sexuality, for most teenage girls, does not have the 'in the air all the time waiting to be attached to anything' quality that it has for boys. It does not drive the wedge between child and parent.

In fact, because their sexuality is not such an issue in their relationship with their parents, some teenage girls can maintain a warm relationship with their fathers – that is, if the fathers are not put off too much by other characteristics of their adolescent behaviour. Teenage girls can in fact have a warmer relationship with their fathers than with their mothers. With almost all girls, the attachment to the mother is stronger than the one to the father, and therefore the adolescent mandate requires much more negativism in order to deny that tie with the mother.

Teenage girls also argue far more than boys do as an outgrowth of earlier styles of fighting and relating to peers. Girls can talk about feelings. Girls can have very emotional, even nasty verbal fights with one another. They simply are better at and more familiar with verbal interactions, even when they do get emotional. Therefore girls, having had the practice going into adolescence, are far better equipped than boys to deal with the emotional exchanges that characterise their relationships with their parents.

> *'I don't know why you think you're so great, Elaine. You know I've been to your house. You don't even have a washer and dryer. Your family has to go to the launderette.'*

> *'I wouldn't talk, Janice. At least my father still lives at home. You say yours takes you out every weekend, but I bet he doesn't.'*

Battles equal contact

A battling teenage girl can certainly be more of a strain on parents than a disappearing teenage boy. Yet this battling is not as bad as it seems. Though they are disagreeing and criticising, they are nonetheless staying in contact. By fighting, they maintain an ongoing relationship with their parents. They are using their parents for support. Boys are less inclined to do this because they are unable to. As a result, even though girls' adolescence is more tumultuous, at least at home, they also get more support. Girls can have it both ways. They can keep their dependency going via their continuing contact with their parents, however stormy, but they also get to feel that they are independent. Boys, because they isolate themselves and have nobody to lean on, are forced to deal with problems more on their own. They are perhaps more vulnerable to serious problems – hence the alarming rate of young male suicide. Amongst 15–24-year-olds, boys are now four times more likely to commit suicide than girls and a later chapter examines these figures in more detail.

Parents are to be taken for granted

'Mum, can you give me a lift into town?'
'I really don't feel well, Elizabeth.'
'But I have to get a notebook.'
'You can go up the road to the newsagent and get one there.'
'But they don't have the sort I like.'
'Don't you understand, Elizabeth? I'm feeling absolutely exhausted.'
'But, I need the notebook really badly.'

What are they, some kind of monsters? Don't they have any kind of consideration? Do they take us totally for granted? If we could get inside Elizabeth's head, we'd ask, 'You really don't care that your mother is unwell?' And she might answer, 'No, it's her job to take me. She doesn't feel that unwell. Besides, what am I supposed to do? I can't drive.'

Worse yet, adolescents will be sensitive to hurt puppies, to starving children in distant countries, to saving the rainforest or a friend with a problem. But not to us, their parents. They do take us totally for granted.

'What am I, a robot slave?'
'You're my mum.'
*'Do you know how much time I spent driving you
around last week?'*
'What has that got to do with anything?'

They just do not see it.

'Mum, you're selfish.'
*'I'm selfish! You're the most selfish, ungrateful child in
the world.'*

Is she really a monster?

Not all teenagers are so inconsiderate. But many are.
They do take their parents for granted, and nothing can
change that. It is important to let teenagers know when
they are being inconsiderate. Parents should refuse to be
bullied – they always have the option of saying 'No'.
But like it or not, the teenagers' behaviour, though
obnoxious, is normal. Not only is it normal, but it does
not mean in and of itself that they are selfish, inconsiderate people. It is a developmental stage, and it does
change – even before the end of secondary school.

But most important, though their behaviour is
obnoxious, terrible, should be stamped out totally, it is
not bad. It is precisely because their parents have been
good parents, have given them the unconditional love
and support that should be all children's due, that they

can be so heedlessly obnoxious. They will openly admit to this a few years later.

'I don't know how you put up with me.'

But not while they are in the midst of it. They simply do not see it. And though they are truly awful, and should be dealt with as such, they are still children.

Adults as idiots

'Dad, why do you have to blow your nose like that? Nobody else blows their nose and makes so much noise.'

'Have you noticed that Miss Pearson has bad breath?'
'I know. Hasn't she ever heard of mouthwash?'

'Mum, why do you use that phoney voice whenever you talk to Dad's parents?'

'Dad, if you know everything, how come you dropped out of university?'

It is very important for adolescents to begin viewing adults as flawed. Teenagers know that they themselves have flaws – lots of them – and they also know that they're expected to go out shortly into the adult world and survive. The natural thing to do is look for evidence that adults are human and flawed as well. If, instead, most adults are seen as perfect, or nearly so, the adolescent will doubt her own ability to make it once she becomes an adult. She knows that her flaws are not going to disappear over the next couple of years.

Therefore it is particularly important for adolescents to view their parents as flawed. But for parents who have been accustomed to unabated admiration from their children, this critical attention can be more than a little upsetting.

I don't have to put up with it. I am not going to stand for my own children criticising me and even holding me up to ridicule. I am the parent, and I insist on remaining a figure of respect.

Good luck. It is normal and healthy for teenagers to prefer to see adults as fools. However, and ironically, teenagers also want to view adults as good and competent and worthy of respect. They do want to have adults to look up to – if they can find them. But now with their more adult and critical eyes, they see the flaws. What they ideally want to see, especially in their parents, is adults who are flawed but who are not thrown by their own flaws, and hence are still worthy of respect. Adults who act as if they know everything are hard for teenagers to stomach.

*I'm trying to get used to the idea that I'm going to be
an adult but will still have lots of flaws. And here's
some idiot acting like he's perfect, which nobody is.
What a fool!*

To get along with teenagers, parents need to accept that
they themselves have flaws. Even better, adults should
have a sense of humour about this state of affairs. Parents
who do can become a model for their teenage children
because teenagers also have trouble accepting their
flaws.

Parents as an embarrassment

When Nick was in secondary school, his father sometimes gave him a lift to the bus stop if he was running
late in the mornings. The bus stop, where maybe half a
dozen children were waiting, was around a sharp bend
after a relatively straight stretch of road. Nick would
always insist on being dropped off just around the bend
from the bus stop. He did not want the others to see
that he was dropped off. What was the problem? Did he
not want the other kids to know he had parents?

Rachel and her mother were in the shopping centre
looking for clothes. Rachel's mother saw a couple of
Rachel's friends ahead of them. Next thing was that
Rachel had vanished. She eventually found her hiding
behind a display in a toy shop. 'Have they gone, Mum?'

Not only do teenagers view their parents as grossly

flawed, but they also find them excruciatingly embarrassing, especially if they are seen with their parents anywhere outside the home. The adolescent mandate says that teenagers must disown their parents in public and commit to the world separate from home. As a result, parents and the world out there – particularly friends – do not mix at all. Co-mingling between parents and friends is embarrassment beyond belief.

> *He used to love going out with us to a restaurant or to the pictures. We had such great family outings. But now he flatly refuses to be seen with us in public.*

> *It's not that I want to be rude or anything but I feel like so embarrassed when any of my friends see me with my parents.*

> *I can't stand it when my Mum starts asking my friends questions when they come over to the house. Like she's trying to be friendly. I can't help it, but it drives me crazy. And one time she was driving me, Jenny and Lydia to the shops and we were singing this song and she actually joined in. I thought I would die.*

They even look up to some adults, but never us

> *Mum, don't buy any more crisps, okay? The football coach Mr Thurgood says I should cut down on junk food.*

Mum, you should be more like Yvette's mother. She really is great. Sometimes when I'm over at Yvette's I talk to her and she really understands stuff.

Many, if not most, teenagers find an adult whom they like, respect, and even listen to. Many adolescents do crave adult closeness and guidance, but since their parents can no longer be that chosen adult, they often find substitutes, perhaps a teacher, a school counsellor, a friend's parent, or even an aunt or uncle.

This behaviour may be frustrating and even the source of a little jealousy for parents. 'What's wrong with me? I know Yvette's mother. I am ten times more understanding than she'll ever be.' Later on, when they are beyond adolescence and feel separated enough, children can come back and look to their parents for closeness (up to a point) and guidance (up to a point). But during adolescence they often look elsewhere. And more often than not they are helped by these relationships.

Friends are everything
As teenagers turn away from home and parents, they suddenly become much more vulnerable to the world beyond the home. This is where their future lies. They cared before about success and acceptance by friends, but now they care intensely. In order to feel good about themselves, in order to feel secure, they must see a place

for themselves in that world, especially in relation to their friends. Their most intense highs and lows are now dictated by the success or failure of those friendships. Success in the classroom or on the sports field is important, but true happiness for a teenager begins and ends with friends.

Fitting in – Girls

'Hi, Sasha.'

'Oh, hi, Janet.'

'Before you get too friendly, Sasha, I just want you to know that the reason I called is that Jessica, Anna and I were talking and we decided that we don't want you to sit with us at lunch any more. We think that you're not popular enough, so we don't want you sitting with us. So please don't try to eat lunch with us tomorrow.'

'Lauren, Hannah and I want to ask you something.'

'Yeah?'

'Why is it that you sometimes wear jumpers that have stains on them?'

Sarah noticed at lunch that Rachel and Debbie seemed to be talking about her without including her. She had noticed more of this sort of thing lately, and she was upset. That night Sarah launched a counter-attack.

Oh, listen, Debbie, I meant to tell you. The other day

51

I was talking to Denise and she said that Rachel had said to her that although you and she are really good friends, she thinks that sometimes you act really up yourself. Rachel made Denise promise not to tell, but you know how Denise blabs everything.

The whole story was, of course, a total lie. But Sarah hoped that maybe it would help drive a wedge between Rachel and Debbie.

Newly adolescent girls, forced by their adolescence to separate from their parents, are not confident. In time, they may become so. But the young teenage girl feels the ever-present threat that she could lose it all. This underlying insecurity gives rise to much cruelty. At the same time, teenage girls make strong, almost loving attachments to girls whom they admire, which often creates intense jealousy. The result of this combination of insecurity and strong attachments is an unparalleled nastiness. It is most clearly observed in the phenomenon of early adolescent cliques. (This is true with boys too, but not nearly to the same extent.) Little can rival the viciousness and social desperation of 11–14-year-old girls.

The basic purpose of cliques is to give each group member a sense of self-worth, which is inextricably tied to the exclusiveness of a clique. A clique can serve its purpose only by being a clique, by excluding others, by putting them down. 'We are better. Is there anybody else in our class who dresses as well as us?' The nastiness and the cliques existed prior to adolescence. But with adolescence the need to find security and self-worth outside the home increases dramatically. To an appalling degree their day-to-day feeling of self-worth is directly tied to a sense of their own popularity. One wants to be accepted and one also wants that acceptance to be as high on the social ladder as possible. 'After Annabelle Rix, it is definitely either me or Becky who is the second most popular girl in our class. I mean, nobody can compete with Annabelle.'

And all of this transpires on a daily, sometimes minute-to-minute, basis. Where do I stand? Am I perceived as cool? Do they still like me? A girl may take even the most casual remark from a friend at school as a sign that something is wrong. And, until explained, the remark can become an obsession.

'Lisa, why did you say that my teeth looked funny today?'
'I don't know. I didn't mean anything by it.'
'Are you sure?'
'Yeah.'
'Oh. Okay that's a relief.'

A common phenomenon is the teenage girl who simply does not have the toughness to endure the social meat-grinder of the early teenage years and who, in effect, opts out. Such girls will often have mostly boys as friends, and will say quite openly that they simply find boys easier to get along with, more accepting, than girls.

Fortunately, the stage where popularity means everything passes. By the middle of secondary school, girls have usually formed more lasting friendships and are content to be part of a small but secure group of friends. As they mature, the importance of being popular wanes, and is replaced by real, lifelong friendships. But, while it lasts, this can be a very nasty stage.

Fitting in – Boys

With boys it is somewhat different. Popularity and cliques are also part of their lives, but not to the same extent as with girls. As far as friends are concerned, boys generally are easier. As long as a boy is not completely odd, in which case he runs the risk of being bullied, there are not too many requirements for acceptance. Before adolescence the two things that matter are being tough and being good at sport, with the latter probably of primary importance. But what also matters is the ability to be fun to be with. Overall, adolescent boys very much enjoy their friends. Most teenage boys will usually say that 'hanging around' with friends and partying are their favourite things to do.

However, with the onset of adolescence there does seem to come an upswing of competitive posturing. This seems to be the main time when boys have to fight a lot to show who is tougher. Or, more accurately, they have to talk a lot about fighting, with an occasional real fight thrown in.

> *'Tom Granger said that he's going to beat you up.'*
> *'Yeah. Well, he's a fucking wimp. You tell him that*
> *I'm going to beat him up.'*

And maybe they will fight, and maybe they won't. In a few years, the odds on fighting go way down. Fighting is admired less and less until, by the middle of secondary school, it's considered downright ridiculous to fight, unless the boys are drunk, in which case it is more acceptable, because it's part of being drunk, which is fine.

Cool replaces tough. Coolness – the capacity to be in style – is a kind of sexualised, downbeat version of tough. The need to be cool, to be in style, is probably the closest that boys come to teenage girls' obsession with looks. But this concern is different in that it is not nearly so demanding. One does not really have to be cool. Many boys do care about how they look and act, but mainly that caring has to do with trying to get girls, not with peer acceptance. For the most part, how a boy looks and dresses is not so much an issue of status as it is one of identification. How you look and dress indicates which general group you belong to – be it 'rude boys', 'cool crowd', 'Goths', or whatever.

In general, as far as fitting in is concerned, teenage boys have it easier. They are easier for adults to get along with. Even with that apotheosis of teenage uncoolness, the nerd (who is usually a boy), social ostracism is just not that daunting. There are many nerdy teenage boys. That is, boys who just do not seem to care about being in style, or simply do not have a feel for it. And for the most part, they are not unhappy. They usually have a couple of friends, they have interests that they enjoy, and in many ways they have an easier adolescence than their more self-conscious classmates. For social acceptance, boys are just not as demanding as girls.

The tyranny of how I look

Perhaps no other issue of adolescence can be quite so cruel as the tyranny exercised over adolescent girls by their own appearance.

'Mum, I'm not going to school today.'
'What did you say, Charlotte?'
'I'm ill. I'm not going to school.'
'You don't sound ill.'
'Well, I am. And besides, I can't get my stupid hair to look right.'
'It looks fine, Charlotte.'
'No, it doesn't. Ever since I had it cut, it looks all wrong, and today I just can't make it look right at all.'

'Well, I think it looks very nice. Now hurry up or
you'll be late for school.'
'I told you, Mum, I'm not going.'
'Of course you are. You look fine.'
'No, Mum. I'm not going to school.'

Nor did she.

'Mum, I can't find my green jumper.'
'It's at the dry cleaner's, Charlotte.'
'What?'
'I said it's at the cleaner's.'
'But it can't be.'
'Well, it is.'
'But then I have nothing to wear.'
'You have your blue top.'
'It has a spot on it.'
'Well, what about that nice light blue one?'
'I can't wear that, Mum, it makes my breasts look too
big. You know that. I have nothing to wear.'
'You have lots of very nice clothes, Charlotte, I'm sure
you can find something.'
'I can't.'

'Mum, my face looks bumpy.'
'No, it doesn't, dear.'
'Yes, it does. I was just looking at it in the mirror and
it definitely looks bumpy. Come here. Look at it in the
mirror.'

'I can't see anything, dear. Your face doesn't look
bumpy to me.'
'I don't know how you can't see it. It's bumpy.'

Prior to adolescence many girls already care a lot about how they look, particularly as it relates to their feelings of acceptance by other girls their age. With adolescence the greater reliance on peers for their sense of self-worth combines with newly emergent sexual feelings to make 'how I look' take on extraordinary and all-consuming importance.

Leaving the security of home, where there is no self-consciousness, and crossing over the threshold to go to school – where everyone sees you – can be over-whelming.

Didn't Janice wear that green jumper yesterday? I
didn't know her family was deprived.

Aren't Tanya's cheeks fat? I never noticed it before. I
don't know why not. She looks sort of like a hamster.

Girls at school do not always say or think these things, but every teenage girl going to school feels that they do. Certainly they know that they do it themselves.

Not only are teenage girls passionately self-conscious about how they look, but also most of them feel they are ugly, or at least less attractive than they really are.

They feel this way for two main reasons. The first is that much of female sexuality is focused not on boys but on themselves, on how they feel about their own appearance. Male sexuality is just the opposite: it focuses most strongly on the object of desire. The second reason is cultural. In most contemporary Western cultures girls are exposed from an early age to a world that says it is a very good thing to be beautiful. Furthermore, television, films and magazines continually reinforce exactly what beautiful is.

Girls know exactly what they are supposed to look like. And once they reach adolescence, the majority of them become painfully aware that they fall far short of their ideal. The concern with their appearance can become a true burden. Many teenage girls get out of bed on school days an hour, even two hours earlier than necessary, just to work on getting themselves to look right.

> *'Caroline, you really are an attractive girl.'*
> *'You only say that because you're my mum.'*

Nothing parents say seems to help. For teenagers, the only thing that matters is what their peers think. Caring intensely during early adolescence about how one looks is normal. And it can even be a source of pleasure. But it can also get out of hand. Anorexia is a psychological disorder where girls (and only occasionally boys) starve themselves, sometimes fatally, in their conviction that they can never be thin enough. It is a disorder that occurs only once adolescence has begun. Prior to having sexual feelings, girls cannot be truly anorexic because the sexual feelings contribute so strongly to the obsession of never feeling quite thin enough. Eating disorders are climbing to epidemic proportions in Britain – and the Mental Health Foundation estimates that one in twenty young women is likely to suffer some symptoms of eating disorder.

The typical teenager

There is no fixed way of being a normal adolescent. A teenage boy may help around the house without being asked, a teenage girl may not argue at every turn, and such behaviour would not necessarily suggest a need for immediate psychiatric attention. But the gender-specific solutions to the dilemmas of adolescence described here are more than just the usual ways of coping with teenage years. They are dictated by very real psychological forces common to all adolescents. Much about adolescence differs from child to child, but much more is the same.

3

Being the Parent
of a Teenager

I f establishing a sense of one's own independence is
the main job of the adolescent, then letting go of
their children is the main task of the parents of adolescents. It is not long before teenagers will be out on
their own, and once out there they must be able to survive. Gradually, whether teenage children seem ready
or not, they must be allowed to take over the controls
of their own lives. But the deepest impulse of their parents screams out against this duty. 'They are too young.
They don't know what they are doing. The world is
different today. It's so much more complicated,
tougher, more dangerous.' Still, parents must let go,
and, to make matters even trickier, they must do so

while still setting limits and making demands. And often hardest of all for the parents of the averagely belligerent teenager, love must still be given.

What is it to be the parent of a teenager? It is to do what you think best – when really you have no idea what is best. It is to ride out the storms and be back again the next day. It is to continue to give love to a child who does not seem to want it, to a child who, five minutes earlier, seemed to deserve a slap more than anything else.

Letting go

The capacity to let go, to separate, to allow a child to pursue his or her own destiny is crucial to being the parent of a teenager. But it is also hard. Parents of teenagers must somehow accept that a lot may go on over which they have no control. Their teenage children may eventually drink, smoke, have sex, use drugs, and there may be little that the parents can do about it. Even less can they control the more generally uncooperative, obstreperous behaviour which is the hallmark of adolescence.

It is during their teenage years that our offspring finally begin to resemble the adults they will become. Often enough, the initial indicators of the future are not at all what their parents had envisioned. We might like to change what we see, but cannot. It's too late. They're already launched. Nevertheless, parents must accept their adolescents for who they have in fact become, rather than 'punish' them for not having become someone else entirely different. Parents of teenagers must tolerate losing a child and, when the last child is gone from the household, become accustomed to suddenly being alone in a new way. The role of active parent that has defined their lives for the past eighteen or so years is stripped from them. Letting go is rarely easy.

Preventing disaster

Prior to adolescence, when a child makes a mistake the worst that can happen is that he will suffer. It's easy enough to pick up the pieces and go on to the next event. But during adolescence errors are not so easily forgotten or forgiven by the world. They can really matter. To do badly in school, to succumb to drugs or alcohol, to become pregnant, all can lead to long-term difficulties affecting the rest of one's life. Mistakes in adolescence not only can hurt; they can cause problems that do not go away. Parents understand this, of course, and therefore letting go during this crucial period takes on a whole new meaning. This is the cruel irony: we are asked to let go precisely when the stakes go up.

Being the parents of adolescents is hard because children may have reached this stage without acquiring the ability to deal with problems at all well. It is one thing to let them fail so that they may ultimately learn how to succeed. It is another thing altogether to let them fail when there is no lesson to be learned, when the only outcome is ... failure.

Some parents when they contemplate all this may have a fantasy solution. When the difficult years arrive they fantasise about restricting the teenager to his room and then checking on him regularly until it is time for him to leave and go away to college, thereby avoiding all the problems. Unfortunately, the average teenager is unlikely to agree to this plan, and in any case social services might have something to say about it!

As an alternative some parents may talk only half-jokingly of moving to a small village in the Scottish Highlands just to get away from all the bad things that could tempt or harm their children. (Of course, villages in the Highlands also have their share of problems.)

But once a child becomes a teenager, he faces risks which simply did not exist before. These risks are heightened by the increased freedom and responsibility that one has to give teenagers, just because they are older, even if they do not seem ready for it. The dangers that exist are real. We can hope to guide our children, to protect them. But, as teenagers, they are out in the real world – a world that has real dangers. This we have to accept. We cannot hold them back.

For a select group of parents the answer lies in boarding school. This has the attraction of removing adolescents during the roller-coaster years and letting the institution deal with many of the conflicts and the

battles, setting the boundaries and formulating the punishments as they see fit. Yet this is only an option for
those with sufficient means and it can indeed breed its
own set of problems. Moreover, boarding schools are
no longer immune – if they ever were – from the classic twin pitfalls of sex and drugs.

Letting them fail

Jeremy had some history course work due on Monday.
He kept putting it off; only on Sunday night did he
finally make a start. By then there simply was not
enough time left. On Monday morning Jeremy said he
was feeling unwell and could not go to school.

'You didn't finish the history essay, did you?'
'No. But that's not why. I really am ill.'
'I don't believe you, Jeremy. You've done this before.'
'But, Mum, if I go to school and don't hand in the
course work on time, it will lower my GCSE mark.
And you know I have to get good grades for university.
Mum. Please. I swear to God, I won't do this again.'

If Jeremy goes to school and does not hand in the
course work, his mark will go down. This could affect
his final GCSE grade and eventually make his UCAS
entry just that much less attractive to a university. It
could make a difference. But should his parents keep
bailing Jeremy out? If they do so, how will he ever learn

responsibility? Unless they let him suffer the consequences of his laziness, how will he ever start to change?

This argument makes sense, but the reality is that
Jeremy may not learn from his mistakes in any event.
He may simply continue to delay course work, be
forced to go to school anyway, and get substantially
lower grades as a result. He may indeed ultimately jeopardise his chances of admission to university. So, should
Jeremy's parents let him stay at home to finish his history course work?

Janine's father noticed that she was often very bossy
when she was with her best friend, Debbie. He com-
mented on this to Janine. But the bossiness continued.
And, in fact, Debbie eventually broke off the friendship.

Janine then found a new 'best' friend, but she was
also bossy with this new girl. Janine's father observed
this behaviour and was tempted to intervene. After all,
his daughter was sowing the seeds for another failed
relationship. But should he intervene?

Unfortunately there comes a time when it is no
longer appropriate for parents to rescue their children.
Sometimes children are going to fail and parents simply
have to let it happen, not because this is the only way
teenagers will ever learn anything, but simply because
it's time for them to proceed with their own destinies
whether or not they learn anything in the process. The
time is long past when parents can hope to manage and
intervene in their children's friendships, which they

may have done when their children were at nursery or primary school.

The problem of separation is not, of course, isolated in adolescence. Within all of us there remains a vestige of the baby self that does not like to separate, that does not like to be independent. For parents, children provide a new source of attachment. And although our children get older and inevitably grow away from us, the process of our growing away from them is not as certain. We get used to their loving us and needing us. They can even become the central meaning in our lives. This can be a dangerous passion, because they *will* leave home. Then what? We may find that we have very little left. Fearing this, knowing this, we can become unwilling to give them up. We can become inappropriately involved in their needs. We can feel that our continuing supervision is necessary to them, while in fact it's necessary only to us.

> *You're wrong. My Sabrina cannot manage without me.*
> *If I weren't always watching over her, God knows*
> *what would happen to her. She certainly can't run her*
> *own life. Ask anybody.*

Maybe Sabrina can't run her own life, but at some point her mother has to let go and let her daughter make a muddle of things. She can hope to guide Sabrina, to protect her, but she absolutely must not hold her back. She must let go.

*But I'm not going to stand by and watch while she
messes up her whole life.*

After a certain point, awful as it may seem, that is
exactly what parents have to do. It starts with leaving
them to sort out small things by themselves.

Sam forgot his games kit and knew he would get into
trouble. He texts his mother, who is working from
home, to see if she could drop it by the school, which is
not far away.

Yet now he is no longer in primary school she feels
that he should accept the consequences of not being
organised or getting up early enough to sort out his
belongings for the day. She is sorry he will be in trouble, but he will have to deal with this small episode by
himself and not expect her to come running. Next time
he will be more careful. And gradually there will be
bigger and longer-term problems that Sam will have to
deal with by himself. His parents will have to hold back
and watch him.

Accepting them for themselves

We love our children and we enjoy them. At the same
time, we have expectations for them. We take pleasure
in their successes and are very disappointed by their failures – not just for them but for ourselves. Our egos ride
on how well our children do. 'But that's terrible. Parents should be happy for who their children are, not for

how successful they are.' True, but feelings of pride and indirect glory are normal. The problems come not from these feelings, but from what we do with these feelings.

Isabel was getting Cs and Ds in her secondary school reports. Her parents wanted her to go to university but Isabel was ambivalent. She preferred to hang around with her friends or, when home, to watch television, use her phone or go on the Internet for hours on end. One day Isabel and her mother were carrying a heavy table up the stairs. When Isabel stumbled, an edge of the table scraped against the wall, digging into the plaster.

'Watch out, Isabel. Can't you do anything right?'
'I tripped. It was an accident.'
'You don't watch where you're going. You're not careful about anything. You don't care about anything.'
'Mum, I'm sorry, it was an accident.'
'You can jolly well pay for it. I work hard. What do you do? All you do is talk on the phone and hang out with your stupid friends. You're not going to do anything with your life. You don't care about anything. And do you know what? I don't really care what happens to you.'
'Fuck you, Mum. You're right, I don't care about anything. I don't care about helping you with your stupid table.'

And Isabel left her mother with the table halfway up the stairs.

'Come back here. Don't you dare talk to me that way.'

As Isabel's mother tried to work out what to do about the table, she also wondered why she had become so angry.

As parents, we have a sense that our children are in a changing state, like wet and still mouldable clay. They are still forming, not yet finished. Their flaws as young children are easier to accept because these flaws may change.

Yet by the time of adolescence there are areas in which the clay has already hardened, where our children have become the final product, the adult they will be forever. A problem for parents of adolescents is that they begin to realise that their children are not so much on their way to becoming something. In some respects they have already arrived at their destination – the permanent adult form.

A Year Five girl who never does her homework and gets Cs is a child who is a lazy C pupil. But a Year Ten teenager approaching GCSEs who is lazy about homework and gets Cs and Ds is someone for whom many avenues are now cut off. She could still go on to higher education or become rich or famous, but her life chances have started to narrow. A teenager who does not care about school and just wants to have a good time is probably not what her parents wanted. 'No, that's not true. I just want her to be happy.'

Many parents genuinely feel this way, but most, deep down, also feel disappointment when their teenagers accomplish little and, further, do not seem to care. We want them to be successful, to be great. Often we want for them the success that we had wanted for ourselves. We may transfer our own frustrated ambitions on to our children. This too is normal. And it is not bad.

Often our children do not live up to our hopes for them. They rarely can, and often we are disappointed. This too is normal and not bad. But sometimes we take our disappointment out on our children. This may be normal but it is not okay. It's not fair on our children to get angry with them because they have not become what we had wanted. That's our problem, not theirs.

To deal with this problem, we must first recognise it as a problem. We must openly admit our disappointment in what they have become. This admission is the most important step, and one that we are often reluctant to take. It carries a certain depressing finality: 'This is it, this ends my hope. I wasn't as successful as I wanted to be and now Isabel's not going to be either.'

We must allow ourselves to feel bad and grieve for what might have been: 'She's not going to be anybody special. She's just going to be Isabel.'

Only after we have admitted to ourselves our disappointment and allowed ourselves to feel bad about it can we refrain from taking out our feelings on our children. And that is the only fair thing to do.

Dealing with the day-to-day
Setting limits

Let me try to explain it. It's not that I hate my parents. It's not that I think they are bad parents. I know they love me, and that what they do they really think is in my best interest. It's just that I feel trapped.

I know that I'm young and that my judgement is not perfect and that I'm going to make mistakes. But they make mistakes too. And I'm not a little child any more. I have a brain and I've been through a lot. There was a lot of stuff that I went through, and they weren't involved at all, and it turned out all right in the end.

The problem is that I can't stand them always telling me what to do. I can't stand that there are rules, even if I break them.

You don't know what it's like. When I'm alone in the house, I'm happy. I don't do anything wrong, at least nothing really bad. But as soon as they walk in the house, I hate the place. It's like suddenly there's a weight pressing in on me. I'd run away, but where would I go? I would love, really love, to have a flat of my own. I could manage. They'd be surprised.

*And then maybe I would go to school and maybe I
would't, but it would be my decision.*
    *You can't know how much I want to be on my
own. I would be so happy.*

To be left alone – this is the teenager's dream. Yet is it
a delusion? In general, the judgement of a teenager is
not as good as that of an adult. Adolescents simply have
not been through it before. Even with parental controls,
teenagers will still make bad decisions, but without such
controls there is no question that they would make even
more bad decisions.

However, heading off bad decisions is not the only
issue in setting limits. Teenagers truly believe that they
absolutely do not want controls, and that without them
they would do just fine, but the fact is that controls do
act as a source of unacknowledged security for them.
Total responsibility for one's life is a burden. With total
freedom one has to bear the full brunt of worrying
about making the right decisions. There is something
nice and secure (though, at another level, also infuriating) in the knowledge that there are one or two adults
around who are also making decisions about what is
best for you. Without this guidance the full burden of
responsibility could cause more stress than most
teenagers are able or wish to handle. It's hard enough
being a teenager without having to take on the entire
responsibility for your own welfare.

*That's what you say, saddo. But I don't need my
parents. And if you would all just get off my case, I
would be perfectly OK.*

Teenagers fervently wish that their parents would leave
them alone. They hate their parents' rules and constantly rail against them. They hate their parents' concern.

I'm doing fine. I don't need anyone to look after me.

And yet it is precisely this parental concern which
ensures that their children do not feel alone. This concern is what we can give them in their adolescence. So
long as parents continue to be concerned, to try to look
out for their teenager's welfare, the teenager can still at
least feel somewhat like a child. 'So long as you are
going to boss me around, you are going to protect me
and care about me.' They will not think this, but they
will understand it, deep inside. This knowledge allows
them to keep alive, at least to some extent, the fantasy
that they are invulnerable, safe, under their parents'
wing.

And we do want this for them. We do not want to
force our children to have too little 'childhood', to
grow up too soon and before they are ready. We want
our teenagers to take on increasing responsibility for
their own lives, but not *all* the responsibility. They are

still too young. It is more than they can handle. We do not want them to carry the full weight of the world on their shoulders. Not yet.

Parents of teenagers have an odd role. They fight to control their teenagers, but with inadequate weapons. And after a few years of heated (but at best only partially successful) battling, they give the control over to their children anyway. They are then young adults. So what's the point of those few years of struggle? The point is those crucial few years in which, we hope, our children will mature. Regardless, they will be out on their own all too soon.

Making decisions

Alice was supposed to get a lift home from the party at Karen's and be back home by 11.30 p.m. At 11.20, Alice rang.

> *Hello. I'm just leaving the party. Can I sleep over at Lisa's house?*

This irritating teenage habit of forever changing arrangements at the last minute is all too familiar to most parents and the mobile phone has only made it worse! But in this case Alice's parents know Lisa. They have nothing against Alice staying at her house. On the other hand, this request is a sudden change of plan. Why couldn't she have made the arrangement before? Is there something else going on? For example, is Alice really trying to stay at the party until much later? What is the right thing for Alice's parents to say?

Let me know quickly [Alice adds], the battery on my phone is running low.

At the last minute, Ben gets tickets to the Snow Patrol concert, one of his favourite groups. It is a school night and his parents know that the next day he has a history exam. Should Ben's parents allow him to go?

What is the correct time to expect a 14-year-old to come home from a Friday-night party? 9.30? 10.00? 10.30? None of these?

A problem with raising teenagers is that you are constantly put in the position of having to make on-the-spot decisions, without having the vaguest idea as to the appropriate response – especially if this is the eldest child. Furthermore, any decision that goes against the teenager holds the threat of an immediate, unpleasant and protracted scene.

An important key with teenagers is understanding that it is often impossible to know what the best course of action is, or even whether there is an objective 'best course'. Yet a parent nonetheless has to make decisions, and quickly. You are left with the 'least worst'.

Yes, you can stay overnight at Lisa's.

or

No, you have to come home right now.

And if the latter decision, a protest will invariably follow.

No, Dad. I'm just going to be at Lisa's. You're being unreasonable.

Parents cannot always know what is best. No one can. They will make mistakes. But who better than they to be making decisions about their own child's life? They are the experts on their own child and they, more than anyone, have their child's interest most at heart. Ultimately, parents must base a decision on what they feel comfortable with, and then stick to it firmly. They alone have the task of making decisions regarding their children. That's the job. Parents cannot always be right; they can only do their best. Most important of all, in many situations it does not matter what actual decision parents make. The key is to do what they think is right, and then adopt a firm, positive posture.

The problems arise when parents chop and change, waver or get defensive. Then the teenager, recognising uncertainty, moves in for the kill.

*'I don't know, Jenny, you decide. What do you think
is an appropriate curfew for you on Friday nights?'
'Four a.m., except if it turns out that there's a really
good party. Then I don't have to come back until the
next day.'*

Being a strong parent does not mean that one cannot
reverse a decision. Parents can change their minds. The
trick is in making certain that this about-face is seen as
an autonomous, thoughtful decision, not as a result of
being bullied. There can be a fine but significant line
between the two. It is okay to be swung by a child's
arguments. But the change should come because of the
content of the argument, not because of the desire to
avoid a hassle.

*Oh, Dad, I'm not going to do anything at Lisa's. You
just don't like me to change arrangements. That's no
reason. Please can't I stay at Lisa's?*

Maybe Alice's father does decide that Alice is right. He
just dislikes an alteration of plans. And maybe he is not
worried about her staying over at Lisa's. If so, he loses
nothing by changing his mind.

The problem comes with children who know that
they can bully their parents. Given the opportunity,
they will do just that, time after time.

*'Don't ignore me, Dad. It's not fair and you know it.
You always let Kevin stay out later.'
'Alice, we've gone through all this before. I don't want
to talk about it.'
'You don't want to talk about it because you know
you're wrong. And I'm not going to stop talking about
it until you change your mind, because it really is
unfair. I can't believe you're doing this to me. I can't.'
'Alice, please try to be reasonable.'
'Reasonable? You're the one who's not being
reasonable. You are just being so unfair.'
'Now, Alice.'
'Yes, you are. You are so unfair. I can't stand it.'
'Oh, all right, Alice. Have it your way. But there had
better not be any funny business about this.'
'Thanks, Daddy. I love you a lot. I'll call you in the
morning when I need to be picked up. Byeee.'*

Children of parents who cannot be bullied will also argue, and they too will push – but not nearly so hard, because they have learned that it won't work with their parents.

How does a child know whether a change resulted from her bullying or from a parent's independent decision? In any given instance, she may not. But over time, over repeated instances, children learn whether theirs are parents who make decisions based on what they think is best or on what they think their children will accept without a tantrum. And they will not forget it.

The key in decision-making is that parents make decisions and that these decisions are their own, right or wrong.

But sometimes I just don't have the time or the will. I know I shouldn't, but I give in to her rather than get into a huge fight. I let her win because I just don't have the energy.

This is the truth. The rule about not letting oneself be bullied is not an absolute rule. On occasion, with very persistent teenagers, parents just do not feel like 'getting into it' day after day. Life is too short. If the issue is not crucial, you can concede in order to avoid yet another onslaught of teenage abuse. In fact, if you're not up to a battle it is often better to avoid that route altogether, rather than entering the argument only to get worn down in due course.

However, parents must not *always* avoid the fights. To do so is to abrogate the role of parent. Parents are free to pick the times and issues on which they will make a stand. In fact, there must be times when they do just that. And when they do, fights will inevitably follow. The trick is to save big guns for big battles.

Gentle nudges
But a parent's role is not always to keep the teenager under control; sometimes it is to give him a little push.

Jonathan had been talking about trying out for the local cricket team, but clearly he had mixed feelings. He liked cricket very much, but he was a marginal candidate for the team. He dreaded the humiliating possibility of being left out of the team. The registration was scheduled for Saturday at 1 p.m. At 10 a.m. he announced he was not going.

'I don't have the right form to fill out. You can only get the forms during the week. I can't go.'
'Yes, you can, Jonathan. I'm sure that they can work something out.'
'No, they won't let me. They said anyone who wanted to try had to bring the form. I can't go.'
'Jonathan, if you want to try out for the team, I'm sure it will work out.'
'No, I'm not going.'

Jonathan's parents, however, did not back off, and they finally convinced him, over his objections, to go and register.

Jonathan, you have nothing to lose. The worst that can happen is that they won't let you put your name down.

They did work something out. Jonathan got into the team, barely, and he was happy about it.

One reason for children's success is that they have parents who have cared all along the way about their succeeding and have constantly communicated this caring. Jonathan's parents knew how much he loved cricket, felt pretty sure he could make the team, but also knew he needed a gentle nudge to get past his lack of confidence about trying out.

Other parents do more than just nudge. These are the proverbial tennis mothers, football dads, parents who forever prod, who tell their children, explicitly or otherwise, 'I want you to do well in school and move yourself up the way I was never able to do.'

These are not bad parents. Successful adults often genuinely thank such parents, recognising that had they not been pushed; they would not have been so successful. But the prodding can be a two-edged sword. While pushing often yields positive results, there are risks. Sometimes, children who have experienced success choose to stop achieving. They are pushed too hard.

I don't understand. Right in his final year he dropped rugby and just hung around with his layabout friends. He could have played for the county or better. How could he do this to me?

If we hang our hopes on our children, we must be aware that it is a burden for them.

*I don't really care so much about how I do, but I don't
want to disappoint my Dad.*

In the end everything may work out, with everyone
happy. But if what we want is not just for them but for
ourselves as well, we must recognise this. We must
beware of sacrificing our children to our own unful-
filled dreams.

Giving too much

It is appropriate to make sacrifices of one's time and
energy for one's children, but only up to a point.

Giving is fine and often necessary, but parents who
run themselves ragged doing things for their children
may be setting themselves up for disappointment. A
problem with giving too much of oneself to a teenager
is that if she does not pay you back – and often adolescents do not – a parent can feel very let down. And this
can make for trouble, because parents may become
extremely hurt and upset.

*I just don't care about Debby any more. I look at her
and I feel nothing. After all that I have done for her,
this is how she repays me. She has hurt me so much.*

This attitude is unjustified, a sign of a parent who let
matters get out of hand.

Parents are sometimes allowed to refuse their teenage

child's request. There may be times when a teenager has been so lazy and/or obnoxious that her parent is just too angry to do any favours.

> *Drive you to the party? I wouldn't even sit in the same car with you, Flora. Just get away from me. I'm fed up with the sight of you.*

Teenagers will survive such refusals. It also reminds them that you're human and that humans can get quite angry if pushed by very obnoxious teenagers. This is a useful lesson for teenagers.

Adolescence is a time of increasing separation between parent and child. The parents who do too much for their child may ultimately get in the way of that process. Too many gifts come with too many strings that bind parent to child. Parents need to know when to say 'No'.

Calming the waves of hysteria

But again, perhaps the hardest part about being the parent of a teenager is that though parents must let go, they must also be there to provide love and support.

Fourteen-year-old Julia had been invited to a party at her friend Shona's house on Friday night. However, her parents had already made a family arrangement to see her grandparents.

'*But I can't miss the party. I have to go.*'
'*Nobody has to go to a party, Julia. There will be other parties. We haven't had supper altogether at Grandma's house for ages.*'
'*But you don't understand. Everyone is going to be there. I can't miss the party. I just can't.*'
'*I am sorry, Julia. But I am not going to discuss it further. You will come with us on Friday night.*'
'*No, Dad. I can't. Dad! Dad! I can't! I have to go to Shona's party!*'
'*No, Julia. You're coming with us.*'
'*DAD!*'
'*For God's sake, Julia. It's just a party.*'

Not to Julia. It is far more than that. Missing out on the experience seems a life or death issue.

Teenagers have a lot of trouble seeing past the here and now. Because they have only just started what they consider their adult life, they simply do not have the experience that comes with living. Thus, they lack one crucial piece of wisdom: nothing makes such a big difference. They do not yet know that somehow things almost always have a way of working out – although how that may be seems incomprehensible at the time. The tomorrows keep coming, never so dramatically different from the todays and yesterdays. But teenagers can get obsessively hung up on the dilemmas of now. It is a real and a serious problem. Take Julia in regard to her party:

All of my friends are going to be there. If I don't go,
then everybody will have been there except me. It's like
I won't be part of what's going on. And then at school
on Monday, they'll talk about the party, except I
won't have been there. I'll be out of it. And then
maybe because I wasn't there, they'll think I'm a baby
or something, and maybe they won't be friendly with
me the way they were before. I mean, they'll still be
friendly, but I won't be in with them like I am now.
You see, I have to go, or lose everything.

Teenagers' lack of perspective can be alarming. Here parents have an important role. Since they do have a better sense of reality than their children, they need to keep stating what that reality is. It can make a difference.

'You will not lose your friends because you don't go to
one party.'
'I will! I will! You don't understand.'
'No, Julia, you will not lose your friends. They will
still like you, even if you miss the party.'

And maybe Julia will hear some of this. And maybe she will be reassured.

The unconditional deal
The behaviour of some teenagers can be so horrible and so disruptive that they may need to be moved out of the

home. We will discuss these extremes later on. Most adolescents are just 'normal horrible' and they still deserve our unconditional love.

We may often shout at our adolescent children when they are obnoxious because we do not like it, and we do not want them to act that way, and we want to let them know that being obnoxious towards us is unacceptable. But another part of us says that it is still okay. Although we might hate their obnoxiousness, we may nevertheless defend their right to be that way. They are still children, our children. And we will love them regardless, unconditionally.

I never used to act that way

'Ruth, would you please come into the kitchen and help me with the washing-up?'
'Why should I? You are always on at me and I am feeling really worn-out tonight.'

Ruth's mother hears this exchange and a voice in her head comments:

'I never used to behave that way when I was her age. When Mum would ask me to do something like that, I always did it. Perhaps I didn't like doing it, but I always did it. I don't understand. I just don't seem to be able to control Ruth and Johnny in the way that Mum could control us.'

And, of course, her own mother, who now lives ten minutes away, comments on this too:

> *'I don't know what your problem is, Edith, the way*
> *you let Ruth and Johnny talk to you. We never let*
> *you and Richard talk that way.'*
> *'But I don't let them talk that way, Mum.'*
> *'Well, you must be doing something wrong.'*

Parents of teenagers today have an ongoing sense of not really being in control of what's going on. 'I deal with it, but I am really not sure that I am doing anything right.'

With most teenagers, nothing *does* go terribly wrong, so the day-to-day sense of inadequacy is tempered by the thought: 'Whatever I might be doing wrong can't be too serious.' But even with those parents whose teenagers seem to be functioning just fine, there often remains an ongoing lack of true confidence about one's skills. We live in an age of insecure parenting. These parents are doing quite well; they just do not realise it. Why?

For one thing, today's teenagers do face 'new' challenges that parents feel are constantly lurking. Drugs are a relatively new problem. Teenagers do have sex earlier (although most of today's parents were members of the first generation for which the rules about sex began to change).

But the main reason for parental uncertainty is their memory of their own childhood. When most parents think back they remember, correctly in many cases, that they did not behave towards their parents in the way that their children behave towards them. They were obedient. They did not talk nearly as boldly as their own children do. From this comparison parents often conclude that the difference is their own failure as parents. To make matters worse, the living presence of one's own parents may act as a reminder of this.

Maybe you just don't notice it, Elaine. I know you and Charles would never have behaved like your children.

But parents' comparisons with their own adolescence are usually not valid. Today's teenagers do have more of a general sense of entitlement — an entitlement that includes talking back — but they feel this way because their parents and society at large have chosen to let them. Many of the boundaries which existed a generation ago have gradually disappeared. Hence the sense of uncertainty which the parents of contemporary teenagers so often describe.

So comparisons with adolescence past may suggest that parents of today are doing a lousy job, but the comparisons ignore the fact that it's a different ball game today, and it was parents themselves who changed the rules.

It is harder, it does require more effort for the parents of today to get the same nice behaviour from their children as their parents elicited. But the question of how today's adolescents will turn out as adults is a separate matter. It is crucial for parents to continue to demand of their children what they believe is appropriate. In the short term their teenagers' behaviour may not match their own at the same age, but in the long run, as long as parents continue to make the appropriate demands, their children should turn out just as well.

PART TWO

*Between Parent
and Teenager*

For those who have never brought up a teenage child, it is hard to imagine the day-to-day swings between crazed frenzy and genuine tranquillity. Some of the time, things are calm, even blissful. You love your child and he or she seems just fine. But at other times, perhaps five minutes later, you behave like a wild person, enraged beyond reason, and at the same time you feel certain your child is utterly doomed, so warped in character development as to stand no chance of making it in life. And then things are fine again.

Crises can arise with dizzying suddenness, seemingly out of nothing. Parents can feel very much on the spot, needing an immediate strong and correct response, but having no idea what that response should be. Teenagers feel that they would be fine if parents left them alone *forever*, but parents feel that curfews must be set, schoolwork completed, phone bills acknowledged, dirty clothes picked up, and siblings restrained from beating each other into unconsciousness. 'How on earth do other parents cope with this?'

It is often difficult to know the correct thing to do, and often even more difficult to do it, especially when you feel enraged, betrayed, belittled and depressed. And then the next day comes and Emma seems fine and you can't remember exactly what the problem was.

4

Communication and Trust

Surely, communication and trust are the foundation of any parent–teenager relationship. Or maybe not. The adolescent mandate demands that teenagers separate from their parents.

Adolescents, especially boys, want to say little to and hear less from their parents. And in order to keep their parents out of their lives, teenagers can be very devious about what they are doing. Yet parents are often told that communicating with their teenage children is vital. It is a subject rife with misunderstanding.

Communication

'Well, Nick, what's happening?'

'Not too much, Dad. The usual.'

'How's school going?'

*'Oh it's not too bad, but I'm still having difficulty
with algebra. I just don't know if I'll ever get the hang
of it.'*

*'You know, I felt that way about algebra all those
years ago when I was doing O level maths. I remember
feeling really down about it. But I persevered and
eventually it began to make sense.'*

*'Thanks, Dad, I really like hearing about what it was
like when you were in school. Maybe I'll soon start to
show some improvement in algebra too.'*

The above conversation has never happened. Never. In the whole history of the world. Of course, parents do communicate with teenagers, but usually more along the lines of:

*Don't forget to take the microwave dinners out of the
freezer before you go to school, Samantha.*

Or:

*Eleven-thirty means eleven-thirty and I want you in
then!*

Or:

Mum, can I borrow five quid?

Or perhaps:

Get out of my room!

The fact that communication between parent and teenager lacks both quantity and quality is not necessarily a sign that anything is wrong. Nor is it a danger signal that conversations are often one-sided, with only parents doing the talking.

Listening to your teenager – I

There is a profound difference between listening to one's children while setting limits and making demands, and listening at all other times.

With younger children the rule about listening is fairly straightforward.

> '*Max, Lucy has to finish her project tonight and I would like you to clear away the table for her, even though it's really her turn.*'
> '*That's not fair. You never asked her do it when I had a project.*'
> '*I want you to do it tonight.*'

*'But it's not fair. You never make exceptions for me.
Only for her. Why does she always have to be the one
who gets the special treatment and never me? She gets
out of everything and I never get out of anything. You
really favour her. It's not fair. I never get anything for
me. Only her. Why is it? Answer me!'*

With younger children the rule is simple: in limit-
setting situations, do not listen. If a parent were to then
ask 'Do you really feel that way, Max, that we favour
Lucy?' it would invite disaster. Max would interpret this
as an ideal get-out. 'If I go on fussing, but with greater
passion and length, maybe they will get so mad that
they will send me to my room instead of making me
clear away the table.'

In limit-setting situations younger children will say
anything, resort to anything, either to avoid doing what
is asked of them or to break down a rule:

*I hate you. I'm the only girl in my whole school who can't
stay up to watch* Big Brother. *The other girls think I'm
weird. I'm not going to go to school any more. I'm not.*

The parent simply cannot listen to these remarks. If
your child is bringing up real issues, these will also arise
at another time, or you can ask. Parents make decisions
relating to younger children totally on their own. Con-
sulting with children courts disaster.

With adolescents, however, the situation is trickier. Since they are now semi-adults they must be accorded a new status. What they say – even when the words may be manipulative nonsense – must be given some respect, some validity. It does not do to ignore a teenager completely. But, you say, your teenager doesn't respect you. It doesn't matter. You are the adult. He is the child. Respect is learned where it is given.

> *But, Mum, I know I just got the new boots, but …*
> *Now don't get cross, just listen to me. I can't wear the*
> *same boots when I go out on weekends because it will*
> *look stupid. Everyone will know that those are the*
> *same pair of boots that I wore during the week in*
> *school. They'll think we're poor. It will be so*
> *embarrassing. This other pair of boots I saw are a little*
> *more expensive, but they really are good value.*

Sometimes what they say is nonsense, designed to infuriate, but sometimes it is not.

> *I know it means staying out way past my curfew. But*
> *the main band doesn't even start playing until eleven,*
> *and they're the group I really want to hear. I will be*
> *with Melissa, Danielle and Johnny the whole time.*
> *I've got my mobile and Danielle's father has agreed to*
> *pick us up at 1:15 when it's over. It's totally safe. I*

know that's very late. But I don't have school the next day or anything.

Sally's parents should not necessarily say yes, but certainly they should listen. Sally's argument is a good one.

What should parents do when they have taken a stand and their teenager starts to argue against it? A good rule is to listen up to a point. Listen to their initial argument. See if it makes sense. If it does, genuinely consider it. Parents lose nothing by changing their mind – provided they are not being bullied. But if the argument does not seem reasonable, or if the parent, after due consideration, decides to stay with the original decision anyway, then discussion must cease. Listening must end.

'Carolyn, I'm sorry, but you can't get the second pair of boots.'
'But the ones I have aren't nice enough for weekends.'
'No, Carolyn, you can't get them.'
'But you don't understand. The ones I have really …'

The parent should say no more. If Carolyn continues to badger, just leave. Once a decision truly has been made, swift separation should be a parent's only goal. Nothing else will be achieved by staying.

'You're not listening to me!'
'That's right.'

Listening to your teenager – II

When not setting limits, parents should always be available to listen. Sometimes teenagers really do want to communicate with their parents. They want to tell them of concerns, fears, of things their parents do that truly bother them.

It does no harm to offer: 'If there is ever something that you want to talk to me about, just remember I am here to listen.' Many adolescents may never take their parents up on these offers. But letting your teenage children know that you are available to listen can be an invaluable support to them. And listening means listening, not giving advice unless specifically asked. So if parents say they are there to listen, they must mean it.

'They don't listen to anything I say.'

'Eloise, I think it would be a good idea if you dropped Latin. You're spending a lot of time on it, and you're still not doing very well. I'm worried it's pulling your other marks down as well.'

'No, Dad, I can handle it. Just leave me alone. You don't know anything. I'm doing okay.'

'No, Eloise, you're starting to do badly, and I think the Latin is just too much.'

'Dad! I can handle it. I'm doing okay. Now leave me alone.'

Two nights later:

*'Dad, I've decided to drop Latin. I was talking to
Becky's mother about how I was having trouble in
school and she said maybe I should drop Latin. I think
she's right. Besides, I don't need it anyway, and now
I'll have more time for my other subjects.'*
'What did I just say to you two nights ago?'
'I don't remember.'

This is one aspect of being a parent that is particularly
frustrating. As adults we feel that we are wiser than our
teenage children. We have gone through it all before,
and we know what is going to happen. In truth, we
really can foresee some things to which our children are
totally blind. Little things: 'If you like this skirt and it
fits, then get it. Don't go looking round all the other
shops. You know how you are. You'll only become
more uncertain, and you'll end up not buying anything.' And big things: 'You say you can judge whether
you've had too much to drink and shouldn't drive, but
you can't.'

Teenagers do not seem able to hear us even when we
are right and when our words are in their best interest.
They might listen to someone else, as in Eloise's case,
but they also make wrong decisions and suffer from
those decisions. From a parent's point of view, all the
hassle could have been avoided had the child only been
able to listen. Furthermore, even if it turns out that we
were absolutely right about what would happen and

they were totally wrong – 'Okay, you were right about that. But you still don't really understand, Dad' – this was to them an exception, proving nothing.

To take our advice, they feel, compromises their independence. To take parental advice and, worse yet, to recognise its helpfulness, feels to a teenager like defeat. It is a defeat of all that they are trying to do, to establish that they can make decisions on their own. To have made a right decision because of parental advice is often for a teenager less desirable than to have failed on one's own.

> *What good is it to me if it's not something I worked out on my own? The last thing that I want is for my parents to be right, for them to be helpful. I don't want to need them.*

What can we do? We should keep trying. Parents should give advice. If they see possible trouble, they should warn against it. Although teenagers cannot tolerate listening to advice or following it, they may heed it nonetheless. Sometimes good advice may slip through. Parents do have some influence over their teenagers, though not nearly as much as they would like. As adolescence wanes and teenagers' independence is established, once again they will hear us. But not until then.

'They think I'm always criticising (them).'

'Ben, will you be going out later?'
'I've done all the homework that I'm supposed to do.
You don't always have to check up on me.'
'What?'
'For goodness' sake. I've done everything I'm supposed to.'
'No, Ben, I wasn't thinking of anything like that. I
just wondered if you were going anywhere near the
shops, could you pick me up some disposable razors?'
'Whatever, Dad.'
'No, really, Ben.'

'Why are you looking at me like that, Mum?'
'Like what, Sophie?'
'You know like what. You're giving me that look that
says you're pissed off about something. I can tell what
you're thinking.'
'Honestly, Sophie, I wasn't thinking about you at all.
If you must know, I was thinking about socks.'
'Sure, Mum.'

It is common that adolescents are not only self-obsessed
but that they often assume critical thoughts on the part of
their parents when their parents had no such thoughts at
all. As a result, parents often find themselves in very frustrating conversations with their teenage children, who
seem totally unable to hear what they are saying. It is as
if their children are hearing some other voice.

'But, Rachel, I really don't mind if you go with Katie or not.'
'You don't like her because she gets bad results.'
'I didn't even know she got bad results.'
'But now you do mind. Right?'
'Rachel, don't put words into my mouth.'

One consequence of teenagers' turning away from their parents is that they no longer really hear us. Instead they hear a little voice in their head that they think is ours but is not. It is their version of us. Actually, it is their new teenage conscience, only they do not know this yet. This conscience does not talk with their own voice, as it will by the end of adolescence, but with ours.

The voice they hear is often an inaccurate reflection of our thoughts. Their conscience was formed gradually over the course of childhood. Our voice was part of that formation, but much of a child's conscience develops independently of his parents, and by adolescence much of it may have little similarity to how we think.

Often the teenager's own conscience can be stricter and more demanding than the parents'. Some teenagers drive themselves far beyond our expectations, especially in school or in sports. Others reject the overly strict voice of their conscience, which they believe is ours but isn't.

Fuck all of them. I'm sorry I can't be Mr Perfect like they want. From now on I'm gonna do what I want, and if they don't like it, fuck 'em.

Part of adolescence is the development of one's own set of values. It is a sorting-out process, deciding what to accept from the parents' values and what to reject. The finished product at the end of adolescence is a set of values that is distinctly the teenager's own. But, early on, that process can be very confusing. Inevitably it can include stupid battles in which children fight about things parents never said and in which parents seem totally unable to correct this confusion.

Is communication impossible?

Contrary to the more general rule, sometimes parents and teenagers can and do talk, and such communication can be a positive experience for both.

It was weird. Dad and I were driving down to Aunt May's to pick up a desk and we just started talking. About all kinds of stuff I never talk to Dad about. I mean, I saw him as a normal person. I liked it, but it was weird.

The only problem is that it's hard to make such talks fit into any specific time frame. They happen when they happen. Planning to talk is a good idea, but parents

106

must be ready to accept that such episodes do not usually work out as they wish.

> *I'm sorry, Mum, I really do want to talk to you, and I do appreciate your wanting us to communicate, but I'm just not in the mood for it at the moment. Maybe tomorrow, okay?*

Alas, these breakthroughs in communication are impossible to schedule, but can happen at the most unlikely times.

Trusting your lying teenager

Trust is the foundation of the relationship between parent and teenager. Parents must be able to trust their children. Adolescents must feel trusted, for it is a key to their sense of self-respect.

This credo sounds reasonable but the words have little application to real life with teenagers. Trust is to adolescence what fairness is to childhood. Teenagers, truly believing in their cause, make trust the number one issue with which they hit their parents over the head. And on this issue parents really are vulnerable, because they also truly feel that trust is important:

> *If we can't trust them as adolescents, when can they be trusted?*

That's right. They have to trust me now. It really is
important to me that they trust me. It's a way that
they can show that they understand that I'm not a
young child any more, that I am older.

Those are valid points. The reality of adolescence, however, is that a lot of lying and sneaking around goes on.
Teenagers lie regularly about the details of where they
are going and what they are going to do. They also do
many forbidden things which elude their parents' discovery. About those infractions there's nothing parents
can do. The issue is what to do when you do find out.

Fifteen-year-old Justin received warning notes in
English and Physics. He was supposed to bring them
home, get his parents to sign them, and then return the
notes to school. Instead he threw them away. Two
weeks later the school rang to ask why the warning
notes had not been returned.

'Justin, I got a call from your school today and
apparently you're in danger of failing your English and
Physics assessments. You never brought the warning
notes home.'
'I dunno, they never gave them to me.'
'Justin, you're lying.'
'They never did. They're supposed to give them to me,
but they never gave them to me. My form teacher must
have forgotten. I don't know. I never got them.'

*'Of course you did. That's ridiculous. The school said
they were given to you.'*
'I didn't get them, Dad.'

On Friday evening 16-year-old Lisa said she was going
to Beverly's house for the night.

*It's just going to be me and Sarah and I think Kristen.
I'll call you in the morning if I need a lift home.*

By chance Lisa's mother called Lisa on her mobile but
could not get through. She wanted to remind Lisa of a
hairdresser's appointment the next morning. So instead
she rang Beverly's house.

*No, sorry, Lisa and Sarah aren't staying here. Lisa
said you knew that they were going to a party at
Carrie's.*

Confronted by her furious parents the next day, Lisa
explained:

*'It came up at the last moment. Yes, I did try and ring
you, twice, but no one answered. Then I didn't know
what to do, so I thought it would be okay. I didn't
know that Carrie's parents weren't going to be home.
Anyway I couldn't leave once I got there. Besides, I
wasn't doing anything wrong. I wasn't drinking. Only*

Sarah was.'

'I can't believe you can stand there and lie right to our faces. We were at home all evening. In any case you could have texted one of us.'

'Well, it just rang and rang. I did try and call.'

'You planned it the whole time. You knew we wouldn't let you go, and you lied to Mrs Pendleton as well.'

'I did not. She must have misunderstood.'

'You're incredible. You just lie and keep lying. How can you do this? Do you think we're idiots? How can you just stand there and lie like that?'

'You don't believe anything I say. You don't trust me.'

'Don't trust you? Don't trust you?'

'I'm not lying!'

'I don't know what to do with you.'

'Fuck off, I hate you.'

The problem is that teenagers (in fact, all children) lie a lot, especially when they have been discovered doing what they were not supposed to do. Sometimes they continue to lie even when the facts are undeniable.

He still said he never saw the warning notes, even after we found them crumpled up in his wastepaper basket.

Just as long as they think they have even a remote

chance of being believed, they will lie. They will become outraged when they are telling the truth and are not believed, and just as outraged when they are lying. It is a paradox. They know they are lying, of course, but are still furious at their parents for not believing them.

> *You don't trust me. I can't believe you don't trust me.*
> *I'm going to be 17 in June. I cannot believe that you*
> *are saying this to me.*

> *It's not the point that I'm lying. I'm old enough now*
> *that they should respect me enough to trust me.*
> *Whether I was lying or not has nothing to do with it.*

If the trustworthiness of teenagers is the foundation of integrity in our society, we are in big trouble. Like it or not, lying is a part of being a child. Parents were not so trustworthy as teenagers either, and while we are at times devious as adults, most of us turned out not all that bad.

Lying is undoubtedly bad. But it is also the normal response of the vast majority of teenagers, either to cover up a wrong or to manipulate a situation in order to advance their cause. But for parents to get too caught up in the issue of lying can become a snare, leading to long harangues that go nowhere. The lies can take precedence over the problem at hand, namely, whatever the teenager did that was forbidden. Don't focus on the lying and lose sight of the more immediate and usually more important issues.

In the case of the boy who did not give his parents the warning notes, the main problem was not that he lied, but that he was failing two subjects in school.

As for the girl who lied her way to an out-of-bounds party, the main problem, well known to parents of teenage daughters, is trying to keep track of their daughters. The lying is assumed. And since parents cannot keep a teenage girl at home every night, they have to become especially adept at getting the facts as best they can before deviousness can occur, making sure that they are on the ball when teenagers are being economical with the truth.

> *'Wait a minute. You never mentioned before that Sophie had an older brother who drives ...'*
> *'Yeah, well, it's not exactly her older brother. He's kind of like a good friend who she thinks of like a brother ...'*

Parents may feel that their daughters lie more than their sons, and this may well be the case. But there's a good reason for this. In general, boys do not have as great a need to deceive and lie because typically they are under looser supervision and can get away with their ploy of providing no information at all. Many girls have to lie in order to even things out. It's the only recourse they have. Unfortunately, it can be rather draining on their parents. In theory, mobile phones should make it easier for parents to keep track of their children, but of course it does not always work like that. There is no way of knowing that they are where they say they are, and in any case there are the familiar lines.

'Sorry, I never realised you called … my battery was low … I was out of range.'

In the midst of all this, how do parents actually influence whether their child becomes an honest person or not? The answer is actually simple. If parents are honest in dealing with others, especially in dealing with their own children, they are teaching honesty. If, on the other hand, they lie, especially with their own children, they are training them in dishonesty.

To tell a child to be honest is fine. To be angry with or to punish a child who lies is also fine. But parents should not delude themselves into thinking that these measures teach their children not to lie. They have meaning only when parents practise honesty.

But I don't want my child to grow up to be a liar. By not making a major issue of the lying, aren't I condoning it? Won't she then continue to be a liar as an adult?

Not really. Lying as a teenager is not an especially reliable indicator of whether or not that teenager is, or will become, an honest person. A good part of teenage lying is a function of the strange amorality of the at-home self.

Lying to my parents doesn't count. I really am an honest person.

This may well be true. In any event the fact that a teenager lied to his parents indicates only that he lied to his parents. It does not mean he is on his way to a life of crime. It does not denote a moral crisis. We need to stay on top of what is going on as best we can, but there is much we will not know about, much they will get away with. We should always confront them with their deceit when they are caught, and we must communicate our outrage. But a disaster, a tragedy, such deceit is not. Their slyness may be deplorable; it is also normal, as it was with us when we were adolescents.

What's a parent to do? While it is good to trust one's children, it is also exceedingly foolish to do so in an area where they have already shown dishonesty. Trust should not be a blanket issue. Experience teaches us that it is appropriate to trust teenagers about some things and not about others. 'I've found that I can trust Katie not to have boys over in the afternoon when no one is home. But we cannot trust her about what she says she is doing when she goes out on weekend nights.'

It is also a major mistake to feel that lying destroys a sacred trust. To be able to trust one's teenager is nice for parents, but more frequently it is a fool's paradise.

'You don't trust me.'
'That's right. Am I supposed to?'
'But it's terrible you can't trust your own child.'
'What's so terrible?'

5

Controlling Your Teenager

You do not win the battle for control with teenagers. There are many things that parents absolutely do not want their teenage children to do – binge-drink, use drugs, be sexually active, play truant, hang around with undesirable friends – but most teenagers do some or all of these on a fairly regular basis. Many teenagers basically do what their parents want. Many more do not – at least, not completely. And there is nothing that their parents can do to bring them under total control.

With adolescents, usually the best that you get is imperfect control. There are rules and they are obeyed, sometimes and sort of. Controlling teenagers is hard;

often you don't win. Yet controls are absolutely necessary.

With the large majority of teenagers, this imperfect control is enough. It is all you need. It is not enough to save headaches and worries. Nothing can avoid that. But, for most teenagers, it will be quite sufficient to get through the adolescent years with both teenager and parent surviving in reasonably good shape.

The parent within

One source of parental control comes from a psychological fact of human development: the adolescent's parents are already a part of him, whether he likes it or not, as the teenager's own developing conscience. Therefore what parents say or do has clear entry into the teenager's head.

What will eventually end up as the future independent adult conscience is formed in part from the gradually internalised voice of the parents. By adolescence that voice, the conscience, is not yet completely the adolescent's own, nor is it wholly the separate real voice of the parents. It is somewhere in between, on the way to being the teenager's own independent conscience, but not there yet.

For the teenager this transition can be very frustrating and confusing. The teenager often hears the parents' voice in his or her own head and does not yet recognise that voice as his or her own. Teenagers hate the voice.

They would like to strangle it, cast it out, get rid of it. But it will not go away, for it is already far too much a part of them. Later, when they are adults, the voice does fully become theirs, and, more often than not, they come to agree with their parents: 'I should never have stayed out so late. What I got away with as a teenager!' And ultimately, as parents, they will make the same requirements of their own children, and pass down their own adult conscience, just as their parents did with them. How often as a parent does one catch oneself saying the same things that one remembers hearing (with great irritation) as a child?

Establishing the boundaries

It is a good idea to have rules.

You have to be home on weekend nights by eleven.

You may not have friends in the house after school when we are not here, unless it is Lisa Farrington.

All your dirty clothes should be put in the laundry basket.

It is also okay for rules to be changed if, as already discussed, it is the parent who sets the changes and he or she is not bullied into them. It is even okay for teenagers to argue about a rule and convince their parents to change it. Rules can be in a constant state of flux.

Okay, you can have Ellie Josephs over after school as well.

But there should always be rules. They do have power. They sit inside the teenager's head and exert a constant pressure. And teenagers can do nothing about these rules – although they would like to – unless the parent abandons them. This is how, without recourse to threats or punishment, parents do exert a very real power over their children.

> *'You stayed out again last night way past your curfew. Do not think for a minute that that is acceptable. Two a.m. is way too late for you to be coming in. I want you in at 11.30, and I expect you to be home on time in the future.'*
> *'I can come home when I want. Eleven-thirty is for babies. You can't stop me.'*
> *'That's right, I can't stop you. But the 11.30 curfew stays.'*
> *'I don't care.'*

But she does care. And the 11.30 curfew will continue to sit in her head, exerting a steady pressure every time she goes out.

> *Damn, my parents are such idiots. Eleven-thirty is ridiculous.*

And with most children, more often than not, the curfew will pull them in on time, or thereabouts. Teenagers choose to give their parents power over them because they do not like the alternative – too much hassling for not enough gains. The alternative would also mean that they would be truly free, truly responsible for themselves, and though any teenager would accept this leeway, we know it is not what they really want.

The conscious voice says, 'Fuck you, asshole. Give me my own flat. Give me money. Give me a cleaner. I'll be just fine. What responsibility? I'm gonna party.' Most teenagers, however, do not really desire such freedom. They have an investment in being good, more or less.

I mean, it's not like I won't do anything. I do drink, and I've smoked weed a few times. And there's been lots of times that I was places when my parents thought I was somewhere else. It's not like I'm good or anything. And there have been times that I've disobeyed my parents. But usually I don't, at least not that they get to know about it.

Some of their rules really are stupid, and they do piss me off. But usually I can either find a way around it, or if it's something that I really don't like, I make such a big fuss that I usually can get my parents to change their minds. But I wouldn't want to disobey them all of the time. What's the point?

I don't want to get into hassles with them. My life is okay. They're not ruining it. I don't want to do anything that's really going to upset the way things are. I just wish they'd get off my back a little more.

Most teenagers know that they have a pretty good deal. Teenagers do not want to disobey their parents. That is not their plan.

Teenagers do not want to overthrow the system of parental control, they just want to get round it.

What all this means is that parents of teenagers have considerably more power with their teenage children than they realise. There are some teenagers who will disobey and there is little that their parents can do to influence them. But if parents confront their teenagers with each instance of disobedience, if they do not over-react to each transgression but keep their rules in place, they will have a teenager who obeys their rules, if imperfectly, and the rules, though tattered in places, will hold up and do their job.

Keeping the rules in place

Jackie, you have to be home by 11.

A rule is stated. This is the starting point for a parent or step-parent, or whoever is in charge. It is the main element of control. The rule must be there, in place, and it must be kept in place. Perhaps the teenager accepts the rule, at least initially, but perhaps she does not. Further discussion only leads to trouble. Maybe the child will obey. Maybe she will not. Getting into a fight with her to demand that she obey before she has actually disobeyed certainly sounds like a serious waste of energy.

In the face of a rule that they really do not like, teenagers often have fits. Sometimes big fits. This is where the issue about separation comes in. If teenagers have fits because they are not getting their way, so be it. The rule has been put in place. The best that a parent can do is to withdraw. This may not be easy, since teenagers not wanting to let go will try their hardest to pull the parent back in.

I hate this house. I'm not going to do anything more that you ask me. I'm going to run away.

A parent must not respond. In fact, tantrums can often be good and occasionally very necessary. It means that the parent has set a rule and stood by it, even though it is one that the child objects to. The essence of firm, strong parenting is the ability to make reasonable rules, unpopular though they may be, and then keep them in place, regardless of the reaction that such rules may provoke. Now that the rule is firmly in place, the next step is up to the teenager.

Obeying the spirit of the law

It was a Saturday night. Daniel was supposed to be in by 11.30. He got home at 11.50. He was shouted at and told that he had better be in by 11.30 the next time. He was not. In fact, he kept coming home anywhere from fifteen minutes to half an hour late. How should a parent react?

The main thing a parent should do is realise that the curfew is working, albeit imperfectly. Daniel is not coming in punctually at 11.30, but the 11.30 curfew is very definitely pulling him in. He is coming in late, but he is not coming in as if he had no curfew at all. He is not coming in whenever he feels like it, at 1 a.m., 2 a.m., or 7 a.m. after staying out all night at a friend's house, and without giving any notice. 'You mean I'm supposed to accept that he comes in late every time?' At some level, yes. A parent should keep the 11.30 curfew in force and should react to every late appearance.

Daniel, you are supposed to be home at 11.30. Ten minutes to twelve is not 11.30. You are going to have to come home at your proper curfew. You cannot continue coming in after it, as you have been doing.

But how far should a parent go, how big should his

weapons be, how much energy should he expend to enforce the letter of the law?

If grounding Daniel for coming in twenty minutes late gets him to obey the curfew more precisely, fine. But what if it does not? Or what if it works sometimes, but Daniel ends up being grounded almost every other weekend because he frequently comes in twenty minutes late. How much parental energy is appropriate to try to get a teenage boy to come in precisely when he is told? The answer is probably some energy, but not a lot.

After all, adolescents can differentiate between the spirit (the intent) and the letter of a law. And often they will obey the intent of a rule; but maddeningly, and at times even intentionally so, just to show they are independent they will not obey exactly. Hence Daniel's deliberate twenty-minute-late arrival. Parents must realise that their rules are working, just not perfectly.

Devious defiance

Once rules are established, teenagers try to avoid flagrant disobedience. The majority of teenagers will shy away from direct defiance. Normally there is a line that most of them would rather not cross. They prefer to be devious. This is when their lying is at its best. Teenagers do not mind disobeying; they just do not want their parents to know about it.

So what. If they don't know about it, what's the problem?

I don't know. I don't hate my parents. I just think their rules suck. But I don't know if I have the nerve just to say no to all their rules and then do what I want. I'd be afraid they'd throw me out. Even if they didn't, it would be unreal. Christina Lowry does that with her parents, and everybody knows she's wild.

Therefore most teenage disobedience lies in the realm of deception or at least of economies with the truth. When confronted by a rule they do not like teenagers will do all they can to get it changed, to somehow get around it, to confuse the issue, or, where they feel they can safely contrive not to get caught, to disobey the rule altogether. They will tell half-truths, lies, whatever is necessary to accomplish their objective. They are not above enlisting friends as aides in their deviousness:

Ring me at home tonight at about 7 and if either of my parents answers, say that you don't need to speak to me, but ask them to tell me that you urgently need my history exercise book tonight. Okay?

The teenage preference for deviousness over open defiance is an important fact for parents to keep in mind. It dictates their strategy. The primary rule in trying to combat teenage deception is that any rule must be as explicitly stated as possible, leaving no scope for misinterpretation.

> *'Mum, I'm going over to Yvonne's after school. Can I call you to pick me up around 7?'*
> *'All right, dear.'*

Later that evening:

> *'Pick you up where? I've never heard of her. I thought you said you were going to be at Yvonne's.'*
> *'Yeah, I was. But then we went over to Rochelle's. Is there any problem with that?'*

If the mother wants her daughter to stay at Yvonne's, she had better make it clear at the outset.

> *'All right, you may go to Yvonne's but I don't want you going on anywhere else unless you first ring and ask.'*
> *'Mum, me and Yvonne are over at Rochelle's. Is that okay?'*
> *'I thought you were going to ring me before you went anywhere.'*
> *'Oh, sorry, Mum. I didn't realise what you meant.'*

They can be pretty devious.

But I can't anticipate everything she's going to do. She's so good at thinking of new ways to twist what I said. Each time it's something different.

It can be difficult. Parents can only learn through experience, but they can learn, and they had better learn if they want a reasonable degree of control over their teenage children.

Okay. Mrs Pritchard is driving you to the cinema. But how are you getting back? ... Lucy's brother? I did not know that Lucy had a brother. How old is Lucy's brother? When did he pass his test?

The clearer you are in the beginning, the more you can pin them down, the better the control you will exert. The less room they have in which to manoeuvre and disobey, the less likely that they will do so. Also, if a parent is very clear about precisely what a teenager is allowed to do, then if he does disobey, he can be more easily confronted with his disobedience without as much risk that he will slide off the hook. Confronting teenagers when they have disobeyed is very important. Confrontations can often be defused by glib teenagers when initial instructions were not adequately clear.

'But I couldn't ring you to ask whether it was okay to go out after the film because there wasn't time.

*Everybody was leaving in a hurry and getting on the
tube and I didn't want to get stranded. And I couldn't
use my mobile from the tube. In any case I didn't have
any credit.'*

    'No, Rachel, I said that if you go anywhere after the
film you must ring and let me know beforehand.'

Direct disobedience

It was Friday night and Elisha was supposed to be home
by 11.30. She did not get home until after 1 a.m. She
had not rung, and her mobile was switched off. What
excuses she offered were flimsy at best.

*We had to take Tania home first and we just lost track
of time.*

Clearly Elisha had not wanted to come home at 11.30
and had not tried to. She had flatly disobeyed her parents' rule. What should a parent do?

    Confrontation is the beginning and the end of what
parents should do when faced with blatant disobedience.

    However, 1 a.m. is not the best time for confronta-
tions. Such after-hours episodes can often yield regret-
table results. At 1 a.m. it is time for going to sleep. The
next morning usually works better.

'Elisha, come down here. I want to talk to you.'

'What?'

'I said, Elisha, come downstairs.'

'Okay. What?'

'You came in after 1 o'clock last night and you were supposed to be in at 11.30. I don't care who else was supposed to be driven home, you knew you had to be home at 11.30. It is your responsibility to keep track of the time and not to switch off your mobile. You may not stay out that late. There is no excuse.'

'Eleven-thirty's too early.'

'We've been over all that before. Eleven-thirty is your curfew on Friday nights and it's not going to change.'

'You can't make me come in if I don't want to.'

'Eleven-thirty is your curfew and what you did last night is not acceptable. We had no idea what had happened to you.'

'You treat me like I was in primary school.'

As discussed repeatedly, the parent, having made his or her point, should now say no more. Any further discussion is counterproductive.

Effective confrontation has three parts:

1. A clear statement that the rule has been broken.
2. Emphasis that such behaviour is not acceptable.
3. A declaration that the rule remains in effect.

This confrontation is the core of parental control of teenagers. Really, parents have little more. It's an effective method, but it only works with those teenagers who ultimately do buy into the system of control, who ultimately do not want to rock the boat, at least not too much. And this includes the majority of teenagers. With most of them the system works.

More or less extraneous to the whole situation are threats, groundings, physical punishment, lectures on motivation and attitude, and even rewards. These means might have some effect, but not usually. They mean little because of two basic facts about the control of teenagers. The first is that the only way to truly control a teenager, or anyone else, is to physically stop them. With small children that is exactly what we do.

No, Cleo, don't put your tongue into the socket.

And we go over and pick up Cleo and pull her away from the electric socket. Unfortunately, with teenagers it gets a little more difficult.

No, Cleo, you may not smoke marijuana.

In a fantasy world parents who really want full-time control of their teenage children might imagine hiring a private detective-cum-ex-sportsman. His job would be to trail around and intervene whenever a rule was broken.

*'No, Cleo, put down that joint.' [He physically grabs
the marijuana cigarette.]*
*'Get the fuck out of my face. I can't believe my parents
actually hired you. You're ruining my life, you stupid
prick.'*

Electronic tagging is a method used to keep track of
offenders. Some versions of home curfew order or
supervised prison release use this kind of model. They
operate as twenty-four-hour monitoring regimes in
which probation officers can keep track of offenders, as
an alternative to incarceration. They can even be pro-
grammed to include exclusion areas so that an alarm is
triggered at a control centre if the juvenile offender tries
to enter! In recent years there have even been stories of
satellite tracking systems or phone devices that could be
used to enable parents to keep abreast of wayward
teenagers. It goes without saying that such methods are
impractical and, more important, inappropriate for most
families.

The second fact is that no threat, punishment or
reward will have any effect whatsoever unless the child
himself buys into the system. The best illustration is this
classic 'you break the rule, you suffer the consequences'
scenario:

*Elisha, you came home at 1 a.m. You were supposed
to be in at 11.30. Now you have to take the*

consequences of your disobedience. You are grounded for
a week.

Simple. Clean. Faultless in construction. But the fact
remains that in order for such a system to work, Elisha
must buy into it. That is, though she may moan and
complain at the grounding, rail at the incredible unfairness of her parents, fuss at how they treat her like a
baby and give her no freedom, it is she and she alone
who empowers the system. Unless her parents were
actually to lock her in the house and hire the detec-
tive/sportsman to keep her in, Elisha could leave if she
wanted to. All she has to do to destroy the effectiveness
of the grounding as a control is to walk out of the
door.

The fact is, if teenagers choose to absolutely violate
their parents' rules, they can.

Parents' greatest error
The greatest error that parents of teenagers can make is
to believe that individual episodes of disobedience entail
total loss of control. Believing this, they often go all out,
sometimes with dire consequences, to re-establish the
control that they have not really lost in the first place.
Escalating punishments ultimately run out, and all that
is left is chaos.

I can't stand this. They won't let me do anything.

Fuck them. I don't care what they do to me. What else can they do anyway?

With any teenager on a given evening the lure of being with friends, being a part of what is going on, may be just too strong to resist. In the choice between obeying parents' rules and not missing out on fun with friends, parents' rules will lose out. Most teenagers will disobey in certain situations, regardless of the consequences.

What can parents do to control their teenage children? They must make rules and they must continually confront their children when these rules are broken. And even if broken, the rules should nonetheless be kept in place. Teenagers will disobey again. There is nothing that will totally stop them. And there are some teenagers who will disobey continually, no matter what one does. Confrontation is an effective control, but it only works, as will anything, with those who ultimately do subscribe to the system of control.

Out of control

What of the children who go beyond the acceptable? What of those who ignore the rules entirely, come and go as they please, and perhaps use drugs, participate in serious drinking, and hang out with friends who are clearly up to no good? What can the parents do with the teenager who refuses to do anything around the house and does badly in school, regularly playing truant from individual lessons or for whole days?

These are the situations when parents may be forced to employ 'get tough' approaches. They may try to enlist the courts or the social services system. Some parents may say to the adolescent, 'You can either live here according to our rules, or don't live here at all', and they will lock their child out of their house, sometimes making sure there are alternative living arrangements, but sometimes not. These measures may sometimes shock teenagers into better behaviour, but often if there is any change in behaviour, it is only temporary.

Parents who seek help through the courts or social services often find that unless their child actually has criminal charges pending for car theft, breaking and entering, drug-dealing, or the like, there is not much that the authorities can do.

Resorting to a foster home is rarely an option. These homes tend to be available only to children who have no viable home to live in. Where there is a viable home, when physical or sexual abuse is not an ongoing risk, foster homes, always at a premium, are rarely used for disobedient teenagers.

Sometimes parents enlist the help of mental health professionals, such as specialist therapists, which can prove beneficial. Or parents can ask friends or a family doctor for the names of counsellors who work with teenagers and their families. It is surprising that some teenagers, perhaps contrary to what one might expect, seem to like professional counselling. Sometimes family problems that are causing difficulties can be discussed in neutral terms. Teenagers can listen and talk to a counsellor in a way that they could never tolerate with their parents. But sometimes, even with the most enlightened of professional help, teenagers remain out of control.

What options are left? Very few. Parents in these situations are stuck with a teenager living at home over whom they basically have no control. He or she simply has not bought into any system of control, and is not likely to.

It is difficult to know what is the best course of action when faced with this kind of situation. Nevertheless, wherever possible parents should continue to hang in there. The important thing is to try to keep the basic rules in place even when they are being continually disobeyed.

> *'You came in again at 3.30. We don't want you out that late.'*
> *'Fuck you, Dad. I'll do whatever I want.'*

The message that the parent is aiming to convey is about concern for their welfare rather than annoyance at their disobedience.

*'I only worry about you because I care. I don't want
anything bad to happen to you. I know you think that
you know what you're doing. But I don't think so,
and I do worry.'*
'Yeah ... Whatever ...'

Parents of such children must endure and they must
wait. In time, one of two things will happen. Their
child may mature and the period of flagrant disobedience may come to an end even as their increased age
allows them more freedom. Or they may remain awful,
unrepentant, doing as they please, and for the most part
unpleasant to be around. Parents now have a choice
because these children are no longer 'children'. Parents
are free to allow them to remain in the home or not.
And often, though it turns out to be not so easy to kick
a 'child' out of the house, this is exactly what some parents must do. But the vast majority of teenagers are not
out of control. It only seems that way.

*I have absolutely no control. They are inconsiderate
monsters. They are going to grow up to be monsters. I
feel like a raving lunatic sometimes, they make me so
mad.*

Yet adolescence ends and most teenagers turn into reasonable adults. *What was that all about? Was it really just a
bad dream?* No.

In the end, what really matters is not whether you are able to perfectly control your teenager, but whether you hang in there through every tough time and come back for more the next day.

6

Conflict

onflict is the meat and potatoes of most parent–teenager relationships. The fact is, most interaction between parent and teenager involves some form of conflict.

> That's the truth. I'm either having a go at him for
> something he was or wasn't supposed to do, or I'm
> yelling at him because I didn't like his tone of voice.
> He only talks to me when he wants something.

It does seem this way. To have no conflict at all is to have either a parent who does not care or a child who is visiting his aunt in Devon. Of course, the reason for so much conflict is that we make requirements of teenagers – to tidy their room, empty the dishwasher, do their homework, get up on time in the morning, be home by a particular time – and very often they don't do it.

But there is so much conflict and so little of anything nice.

Yes, but conflict is not necessarily bad. Remember that always lurking beneath the surface with an adolescent, waiting to make trouble, is the pull not to separate from the parent, not to move forward, not to grow up. This temptation is especially true at times of limit-setting, and an excellent way to cling on is to battle. This is why conflict so often seems to get out of hand and take on a life of its own, far beyond where the conflict had begun, far beyond what it's worth. Parents must see these wars for what they truly are – desperate measures on the part of the child's baby self not to let go.

The art of parenting lies in recognising this dynamic of adolescence and learning how to avoid playing unwittingly into its grasp. The secret of a good outcome lies not in a final resolution – there never will be one if the teenager can help it – but in ending the discussion and walking away. Therefore the aim is not to avoid conflict altogether (which is impossible), but rather about limiting conflict to what is useful and necessary, avoiding battles that are tumultuous, draining and disheartening.

Battles (and what to do about them in general)

Battles are both the essence and the supreme test of being the parent of a teenager. Battles can lead to physical harm. They can cause children to run away or to attempt suicide. Battles can create permanent rifts. They can lead parents to divorce. Nevertheless, battles can also mean nothing and can be totally forgotten – by the teenager – within minutes.

A battle begins:

> *'I want to stay out until 1 o'clock tonight. Everybody else is allowed to.'*
> *'No, Emily.'*

> *'Jamie, please will you take the rubbish out to the bin.'*
> *'I can't. My arm hurts. And besides, Sarah's supposed to do it.'*

In both cases the parent wants one thing, and the child wants something else. The child is being asked to do what he does not want to do. More basically, he or she is being asked to accept a loss – not getting his or her way. A loss means accepting bad feelings and this is a signal for action to the ever-present baby self lurking just below the surface, the self that wants only fun, no stress. It decides to make an appearance, thinking:

> Emily: *I don't feel like being disappointed about not being allowed to stay out until 1 o'clock.*

Jamie: *I don't feel like straining myself to lift up the rubbish and carry it all the way out to the garden. What I feel like is getting my way. Then I won't have to have any bad feelings. Yeuch! I hate bad feelings.*

And so the teenager digs in for battle.

Emily: *What do you mean, 'No'? You're crazy. I'm staying out until 1 and I don't care what you say. You can't do anything to stop me.*

Jamie: *I'm not taking out the rubbish. It's Sarah's turn. It's just not fair. I'm always the one who has to do everything.*

This is the crucial part of a battle. It comes very early in the sequence of events. The parents have clearly stated their intention; the children, their defiance. The stage is set for a battle of wills. It is now, immediately, that parents must end their participation. To continue is to be sucked into a trap that inevitably causes matters to go one way – downhill.

The parent can have one last line, but one line only:

Emily, you are to be home by 11.30.

Jamie, take out the rubbish, now!

They need say no more. Their children, on the other hand, are just beginning.

Emily: *I'm not going to be home by 11.30. You can't make me. I'm 15, I'm not a baby. You're totally unreasonable. You are. And I'm not going to do what you say. I mean it. You're such a bitch.*

Jamie: *Sarah gets everything she wants. All you want me for is somebody to do chores. I don't even know if you like me. Maybe I'd be better off living somewhere else. I don't know if you'd miss me.*

These two teenage responses are of course readily identifiable as Tactic 7A – threat of absolute disobedience with accompanying profanity – and Tactic 13B – complaint of unfairness, switching over to grief at feeling unloved. Both tactics plead for parental response. But parents must NOT respond. If they do, all is lost.

You listen to me. You will be home by 11.30 or face the consequences.

Or perhaps, picking up on the abusive language:

Don't you dare call me a bitch.

Or, as with Jamie's parent:

I don't know how you can say things like that. That's ridiculous. We certainly do not favour Sarah over you.

Now the parent has gone one step too far. She has fallen into the trap. Teenagers can easily keep the responses coming.

Emily: *I don't care about consequences. Ground me for a year. That's all you know how to do.*

Or:

Yes I will call you a bitch. Bitch.

Jamie: *You don't realise it, but you really do love Sarah more than me. You don't even notice how much you let her get away with.*

Teenagers do not consciously plan to keep the battles going. It just comes out: the ever-present voice of the baby inside who does not want to let go. For if the argument ends, the baby is alone. And its influence starts to fade. If alone, with no parent to fight with, the child's debate becomes internal.

Emily: *Shit. I really do want to stay out until 1 o'clock. If I leave early, I'll miss stuff. But I don't know if I really want to risk breaking my curfew by*

*that much. I might get into more trouble than it's
worth. Shit. I don't know what to do.*

Internal conflict. Stress. These feelings are part of the
independent mode of functioning and will emerge if
the girl cannot keep the fight going.

Jamie: *I hate taking out the rubbish. It's such a drag. I
know I should do it, but I hate it. I would much rather
stay here in front of the computer.*

An internal struggle ensues between his conscience,
which knows he should do it, and his laziness. But if he
can keep the scene going, he never has to deal with this
conflict – conscience versus laziness – which is precisely
the conflict that a parent wants him to have to face.

Parents must not allow themselves to get sucked into
ongoing battles. It is that simple. They must keep
focused on the issue at hand, state a position, and carry
it no further. Not to do so is to invite chaos.

It is not unusual for parents to lock themselves in a
bathroom to escape children who persist in arguing. But
the biggest obstacle to letting matters rest is not persistent teenagers, but persistent parents. Adolescents are
very good at knowing what gets to their parents. They
become expert at knowing how to keep their parents
going.

I can't let her get away with saying that.

But he really seems upset. I can't just leave it like this.

But you must. There is one immutable fact of child-raising: as long as children can stay in contact with their parents, even through arguing, they do not have to go off on their own. Understanding this prime fact will save enormous wear and tear; ignoring it is to ask for trouble. One of the most fundamental principles of parenting is knowing when to Back Off.

Many doors to doom

They trap us, with each technique more artful than the last. In truth, their methods are not preconceived but are spontaneous urgings of their hearts, unconsciously but unerringly designed especially for us, drawing on their wisdom from all the years together. Their words are all the more beguiling, all the more effective, because of their conviction. Lie detectors would show that teenagers believe what they say.

Here are a few of the most common 'traps'. But no list could possibly cover the unique set of traps tailored to fit each parent's particular vulnerabilities. What follows is a mere sampling of some of the most frequently used.

Teenagers' traps for parents

I don't care.

This trap is particularly effective, as it seems to pull the rug out from under parents' feet.

> *'Stephanie, I am sick and tired of the fact that you think you can do whatever you want. You can just forget about going out for the next two weekends.'*
> *'I don't care.'*

This sign-off begs this response:

> *You don't care. Well, we'll see what you care about …*

The parent, feeling powerless, now seeks greater leverage. The teenager continues with more of the same.

> *You can do anything you want. But I don't care.*

The parent, feeling that she has to come up with something that will have an effect, keeps going. A full-scale battle inevitably results. Which is just what the baby inside the teenager was looking for.

The trick is that adolescents do care. They are just saying that they don't. The correct response to 'I don't care' is no response at all.

Oh yes, I will.

This technique and its companion, 'No, I won't', are much loved by every generation of teenagers and have reduced many a parent to the level of a 2-year-old.

> *'Cecily, you may not go shopping after school*
> *tomorrow.'*
> *'Oh yes I will.'*
> *'Cecily, you heard what I said.'*
> *'I AM going shopping.'*
> *'I am warning you, Cecily.'*
> *'You can't stop me. What are you going to do, come*
> *home from work?'*
> *'Don't try me, Cecily.'*

The trick here is that children risk nothing by saying that they will defy their parents' orders. They may have no intention of disobeying, but lose nothing by asserting that they will. In addition, they may even succeed in picking a fight. And then they will certainly carry on the battle for all it's worth.

I'm going to go into town, Mum. I really mean it.

Having already stated their position, parents need say no more. They should deal with disobedience only when and if it happens. They should ignore all mere threats of disobedience.

You're a dickhead.

This is a particular winner. All a child has to do is direct a verbal attack at a parent – swearing is especially good, though not always necessary for the creative child – and the parent resumes a fight that had been concluded.

'*That's it, Patrick, I am not giving you money for the jacket. I have nothing more to say.*'
'*You're an asshole.*'
'*What did you say? Come over here. How dare you swear at me?*'

And the parent has re-entered the argument. Parents may feel that a particular remark has gone too far, and that depends upon their judgement, but parents must also realise that picking up on teenage jibes risks undoing what may have just been accomplished.If parents are really concerned that a child's rudeness and use of bad language needs to be addressed, they should do it later. In the midst of a conflict, doing so will only invite more of the same.

I can't do anything right.

This example is more subtle than the others, but equally devastating.

> *'Come down here at once and take out the rubbish*
> *now. I am sick and tired of always having to go on at*
> *you. When are you going to learn to take some*
> *responsibility in this house? When are you going to*
> *grow up?'*
> *'You're always criticising me. I can't ever please you.*
> *I'm just a failure, aren't I?'*

If picked up on, this can turn the whole scenario into much more pleasing directions for the teenager, because the subject is no longer the nasty rubbish that needs to be taken out.

> *'You're not a failure, Andy. How can you say things*
> *like that? You're not a failure. It's just that we*
> *sometimes get annoyed that we have to keep on at you*
> *to do things.'*
> *'That's not true. You and Mum are disappointed with*
> *me. You wish I was different.'*

This is a particularly insidious ploy, for both parent and child. Its effectiveness lies in the ability of the child to pull out of himself feelings of sadness and lack of worth which, if they are to be well played, must be believed. And many children can lock into a sadness that has no origin other than the effect that it has upon their parents.

In fact, many children maintain a tie with their parents through sadness. They learn quite early on that being sad or upset can get attention of a special and pleasing sort. Over time, repeatedly using this ploy, they come to believe the feelings are real.

But lots of teenagers are sad. I don't want to ignore him if he says he feels worthless. What if he went on to kill himself after I had ignored him?

The key to parental response is to consider the context of such statements. If you're uncertain, pick a neutral time and ask, 'Andy, do you really feel you're a failure? Do you really feel that we think that you are?' An affirmative answer at that time should be taken seriously. But if the answer is no, parents can safely discount those times when Andy's 'depression' coincides with asking him to take out the rubbish or a similar onerous task.

There are many doors to doom, and some lie within parents themselves. The baby self that does not want to let go exists within every parent too. Once the fight begins it is not always so easy for parents to let go either. But they simply must, because they are the adults.

How parents trap themselves

However, distinct from anything that teenagers may do, there are certain serious traps that lurk within the minds of parents – traps that can ensnare them in fruitless, even destructive, battles with their teenage children.

Correcting character flaws

Probably the most common and most insidious trap is one that makes parents feel that they cannot let a matter drop because their child's very character is at stake.

It was a Sunday and it had snowed. Tom cleared up the front path and the drive. Later that day it snowed a little more, stopping around mid-evening. Tom was in his room lying on his bed, listening to music. His father asked him to clear the path and the drive again. The job would probably take about twenty minutes, no more.

> *'Dad, I already did it. The new snow is nothing. It doesn't need to be shovelled.'*
> *'Tom, it needs to be done. If it's not shovelled you know it will turn to ice overnight – it will be slippery in the morning and difficult to get the car out.'*
> *'Dad, it's fine. It doesn't need to be done.'*
> *'Tom, go outside and clear off the snow now.'*
> *'No, it doesn't need it. If you want it done so much, do it yourself.'*

No matter how you look at it, no explanations other

than bad ones exist for Tom's behaviour. He was lazy and obnoxious.

But this is not an unusual situation. Teenagers often act in ways that are uncompromisingly grotesque and totally selfish. In these situations parents frequently make what is probably the major and most common error in dealing with their teenage children, an error based on faulty assumptions that go to the heart of being the parent of a teenager.

He's so lazy. If I can't make him change now, when is he ever going to change? I can't let him get away with this behaviour. I only have a few years left before he leaves home. It's my responsibility to sort him out before it's too late.

'Tom, you are so lazy. What the hell do you think you're doing? You just lie on your bed all day and listen to music. You can't even do a simple job when I ask you.'

'That's not fair, Dad. I do stuff. I'd do more if you didn't yell at me so much.'

'I yell at you because you don't do anything. I can't believe you're so lazy. What are you going to do when you're older? Do you think you're always going to find somebody to run around after you? I pity your wife. So help me God, you had better learn to sort yourself out.'

Tom rises from his bed and leaves the room.

*'I'm getting the fuck out of here. You clean up your
own fucking drive.'*
'Don't you dare swear at me. You come back here.'

What was Tom's father's error? He believed that since
his child demonstrated major character flaws (rudeness,
laziness), he himself had to act to correct those flaws,
especially since there was so little time left before Tom
would be on his own and no longer under parental
influence. The faulty assumptions were, first, that his
intervention would even have any effect and, second,
that the character flaws so clearly revealed in the snow-
shovelling episode were destined to be part of his child's
character as an adult.

The fact is, if a teenager is destined to grow up to be
thoroughly unpleasant, parental interventions at this
stage are not going to do much to change that. Parents
who try very hard to prevent warped character development in an obnoxious teenager are usually wasting
their time. They are fighting a battle that they have
already won or lost. They just don't realise it.

However, Tom's father compounded his first error
with another error. In his attempt to change a character
flaw in his son he was compelled to lecture Tom on the
consequences of laziness rather than sticking to the issue
of the conflict – was Tom going to clear up the snow?
Teenagers will often use a lecture as an excuse for not
doing something. In this case, the lecture achieved the

opposite of what was intended. It allowed Tom to avoid confronting his laziness.

Lectures do very little. They can play into the hands of the adolescent who doesn't want to separate from the parents. A lecture allows Tom to stay attached by whingeing rather than having to deal with the question of whether he should shovel the snow again.

Parents can rave at their children. They can pull out all the stops in order to change pernicious characteristics. But their energy will be wasted and they will succeed only in producing longer, nastier scenes. Any overall effect will be to slow down the process of maturing.

Only one good reason exists to rave at one's child: it makes us feel better. We should not delude ourselves as to who it is that benefits from our lectures. 'Well. I certainly let him have it that time.'

> *Dad is such a retard. I hate it when he talks like this. Why can't he just get off my case? I really would do a whole lot better if he didn't go on at me so much. I'm not lazy. I would do it if he'd just back off and not treat me like a little kid. He thinks that because I'm his son he has the right to yell at me. I'm not going to do stuff for him when he comes on like such a wanker.*

Tom's father would have been better off insisting on his original request and not getting sidetracked with son-improvement lectures.

'Tom, clear up the drive.'
'No, it doesn't need it. Leave me alone.'
'Tom. Clear up the drive. I don't want to have to
shovel the snow. I want you to shovel it. Now.'
'No. It doesn't need it.'
'Tom, I want you to clear the drive.'

And if the scene is played this way, with Tom's father avoiding lectures but staying with his demand, Tom usually will go out and sullenly shovel the path. Usually, simply staying with a specific demand will achieve its aim.

Just drop it

Getting even. Getting in the last word. Not letting them get away with it. Teaching them a lesson. In the realm of child-raising, these measures usually assure disaster. Can't we just drop it? Leave it there? End it? We're adults, after all. But apparently this is very difficult.

'Simone, where is my white jumper?'
'Umm. It's in my room.'
'I thought I told you that I did not want you wearing
it.'
'I forgot.'
'How dare you keep taking my clothes without my
permission!'

156

*'Mum, I didn't have anything to wear. Rochelle had
borrowed my green top.'*
*'What are you doing lending your clothes to your
friends all the time? Then you don't have anything to
wear and you take my clothes.'*
'Why are you always yelling at me? I hate you.'
*'Don't you dare talk to me that way. Don't you use
that tone of voice.'*
'I'll use whatever tone of voice I want.'
'Don't you answer back like that.'

And on and on.

Why not:

'Simone, where is my white jumper?'
'Umm. It's in my room.'
'Thanks.'

Or if that's too hard:

*'Thank you, Simone. But please don't use my white
jumper again. I asked you not to before.'*
'I forgot.'

Finis.

We can always give a million reasons why we should
not drop it. And usually these reasons sound more or
less reasonable. Typically they involve 'not letting them

just get away with it' or 'teaching them' or 'making sure they learn ...'

But if our aim is not to get caught up in lengthy battles, if our aim is to have them learn something positive, then, almost invariably, the greatest wisdom is simply to shut up. By going on, we teach them only one thing: we want to be in control. And the scene invariably switches from the issue at hand to a much wider battle of wills.

There are, of course, still other traps that can pull parents unwittingly into battles. Many of these involve other family members – siblings, three-way mother–father–teenager altercations. They will be discussed shortly in the section about families.

'How can you ask me to take you to the shops after what just happened fifteen minutes ago?'

Even where parents have the best intentions, battles do occur, and though not usually physical, they nonetheless can get pretty nasty. What may be most perplexing and infuriating to parents is how quickly their teenagers (just like much younger children) seem to recover from such battles. Whereas parents are themselves still emotionally exhausted, their children seem to have totally forgotten about what had transpired only minutes before.

Sarah was supposed to wash all the linen tablecloths and serviettes. Her mother would pick them up after work and drop them off at the ironing service. Sarah remembered the task when she got home from school but kept putting it off, instead watching TV and calling a friend. She had not meant not to wash the table linen, but she had not really meant to wash it either. Somehow she just did not get round to putting it in the machine and switching it on.

When Sarah's mother came home to find that Sarah had done nothing, she became angry. Despite knowing she was in the wrong, Sarah defended herself by saying that it was unreasonable for her mother to assign her tasks in the afternoon, because school was long and hard, and it was not fair to make such demands on her. She had a right to relax after school.

This only infuriated Sarah's mother further, and the scene then degenerated into screaming on both sides.

'You are the most inconsiderate, selfish girl in the world. You make me ashamed. What did I do wrong?'
'I hate you and I hate Dad and I hate this house. I can't wait to get out of here. If you think I'm living here for another two years, you're crazy. I can't stand you. I hate you.'

Whereupon, Sarah ran to her room sobbing and slammed the door. Sarah's mother was upset, but nevertheless prepared supper although she continued to feel shaken. Thirty minutes later Sarah emerged from her room and entered the family room, where her mother, still upset, was reading the newspaper.

> *'Mum, could you drop me off in town after supper?*
> *I'm meeting Yvette at the shops and I can get a lift*
> *home with her mother.'*
> *'What?'*
> *'I said, "Can you give me a lift to the shops?"'*
> *'What?'*
> *'I said, "Can you give me a lift to the shops?"'*
> *'I don't believe you. How can you come in here and act*
> *like nothing happened? How can you dare to ask me to*
> *take you to the shops, especially after what you said to*
> *me?'*
> *'Oh, that.'*

It is a major issue for parents of adolescents. The general principle demonstrated in this dialogue is that from an adolescent's standpoint, most issues are of the moment. They may not be from their parents' standpoint, but they are from the adolescent's. And although teenagers may feel that they mean what they say at the time, they don't really.

> *'Do you really hate your mother?'*
> *'No. But I do when she acts like an idiot.'*

> *'Do you hate your father?'*

'No. I just said that because it sounded good at the time.'

'Do you want to leave your parents' house before you finish school?'
'No, not really. Where would I go? I mean, they do get to me sometimes. But I like my room. And besides, I know my parents aren't that bad. They're just Parents.'

'Don't you care that you say such terrible things to your mother?'
'No. She knows I don't mean it. Besides, she shouldn't have said what she said. She's not perfect either, you know.'

Like it or not, teenagers, especially teenage girls, can become very upset, get very nasty, and get over it very fast. What they say in the heat of battle can mean nothing other than that they are angry. Half an hour after a major blow-up, Sarah can ask her mother to take her shopping, not because she's being sweet and manipulative but because she genuinely feels that the fight that happened half an hour earlier is finished. Her mother got angry with her for something she failed to do, and she got annoyed with her mother for yelling at her. And now it's over.

A parent may wish she could say to a child, 'It's not

over. You cannot expect to act that way and then come back as if nothing happened. You may not talk to me the way you did. You are going to have to learn that what you do and say has consequences.'

The parent may say this and may indeed punish a child for disrespect. What punishment accomplishes, as anybody who has been through this will attest, is nothing. Nothing positive, that is. The same thing will happen again anyway. The speech is effective only in ensuring that the fight resumes.

From the parent's standpoint, the underlying issue in these episodes, once again, is that most difficult of all parenting skills – letting go.

Beyond words

Unfortunately, parents, rather than pulling back, can sometimes get very angry indeed. Angry enough to hit. Some parents use spanking as punishment with younger children. Many parents spontaneously smack their children when they get angry with them. Is this ever justified? It is an issue still wide open to debate. But there can be no argument whatever about hitting teenagers. It should not be done. Teenagers experience hitting, any hitting, quite differently from pre-adolescents. To them it is a physical, even sexualised, insult. Remember that two main psychological features of adolescence are the upswing in sexuality and the mandate to feel independent from one's parents. With adolescence, physical intimacy with one's parents must therefore be sealed off; distinct boundaries now exist between parent and child, and being hit is experienced as a violation of those boundaries. Adolescents react so strongly to hitting that the act is simply unacceptable. In response to a blow, teenagers can become violently upset, so upset that they can do harm to themselves or others. Whether they deserve to be hit or not, one must back off. Regardless of how one feels about hitting younger children, the cardinal rule about teenagers is that one must not hit them.

To complicate matters, teenagers sometimes hit their parents. This too has a different meaning from when they were younger. There should now be a strong taboo against such behaviour inside them. By hitting their parents, teenagers indicate they are seriously out of control. At that point, invariably, parents must seek immediate outside help, possibly even from the police. Teenagers are not little kids, and the act of hitting has the potential of real harm.

Jobs around the house

Coming in when they are supposed to is probably the cause of the most serious parent–teenage battles. But, unquestionably, fights are most commonly caused by a failure to do jobs around the house. This section is about the latter category. Dirty glasses left sitting in the lounge, overflowing bins, chores that get put off forever

– these seem to be the topic of most conversations. 'That's right. I don't have regular conversations. Most of the time that I spend with Darren seems to be me nagging him about something. But what can I do? He simply won't co-operate.'

'Darren, are these your socks?'
'Yeah. So what?'

Of course, there are teenagers who do chores regularly, without any difficulty. But many do not. It is just not possible to get them to do all that's asked. Further, what one does get is often accompanied by objections. Many teenagers can be so caught up in their own immediate wants and needs that they will go through periods in which they will regularly ignore chores around the home, feel only hassled by their parents, expect their parents to do everything for them, and not see that they are doing anything wrong. It remains necessary to stay on top of them all the time unless the parent is prepared to turn into an unpaid servant.

Years ago teenagers, like all children, did much more around the house than they do today, and with fewer objections, mainly because parents used harsher con-trols, and because it was simply expected of them. But, with the major increase in labour-saving devices over the years, the need for help around the house has sig-nificantly decreased. The fact is, teenagers respond much better to need than to what they see as obligation. Teenagers will more readily get up early in the morning to milk the cows, if otherwise the cows will not get milked, than they will move their dirty glasses from one room to another.

> *You don't understand. I have my life and there are things that are important to me. And bringing dishes into the kitchen is just not one of them. If it's so important to her, why can't she just do it herself without bugging me about it? She knows how much I hate to do it. Besides, she's always asking me when I'm doing something else. Keeping in touch with my friends on Facebook may not seem very important to her, but it is to me. It's very important. Glasses going into the kitchen is not very important to me. She just doesn't remember what it was like when she was my age. She must have talked to her friends on the phone in her day. I bet she wasn't so perfect.*

And to say that the problem is that youngsters today are just too lazy is missing the point. Most teenagers, as their confused parents well know, can be incomprehensibly lazy at home but also be a hard and conscientious worker at an after-school or Saturday job. The reason, of course, is that issue of the 'home' and the 'away from home' selves in operation. Knowing this still does not help much when the simplest jobs go undone.

To nag or not to nag?

'I don't want to be always nagging him. But if I don't, then he won't do anything.'

'I try never to be in the same room as her. Anytime she comes to where I am, or I go through where she is, she always wants me to do something. I'm not joking — every time. As soon as I hear her getting near me, I start to get tense. What is she going to have a go at me about now?'

'See? That's just what I'm afraid of. I want us to have a nice relationship, but all he sees me as is a nag, because that's all I ever seem to do.'

'Yeah. Right. I've got an idea, why don't you stop nagging me about stuff? You'd see. We'd really get along a lot better.'

'Yes, that's what I want. But you'd never clear up, and you'd never do anything you're supposed to do.'

'So? That's no big deal, and we'd really be happier.'

'You mean if you leave plates with half-eaten sandwiches in the middle of the rug, or dirty laundry strewn around the place, I shouldn't say anything?'

'Yeah. Try it. I'll pick it up after a while, or you can pick it up.'

'I can't do it. It's too obscene. I can't let him. I mean, his room is one thing, but I just can't let him not do anything. But I don't want to be a nag. I think there are times that he really hates me.'

'It's true. There's a lot of the time when she's really

the biggest pain in my life. I mean, maybe it's a
terrible thing to say, but I'd be happier if she simply
wasn't around.'
'I knew it. I knew he felt that way.'

An absolute fact of adolescence is that if you do not nag,
they will not do what you want. They may not do it
even if you do nag. If having a teenager do nothing is
acceptable to you, then do not nag. But if it is not, you
are stuck with nagging.

There has to be something else.

But what?

You mean if I want him to do stuff, I'm going to have
to nag?

That's right.

Then I suppose I will have to keep nagging.

'I'm going to hate you forever if you nag. It will sour
our whole relationship throughout my adolescence.'
'Tough.'

'I'll do it later.'
If a parent wants something done, he had better make

his child do it right away. Otherwise, the odds are it will not get done, and the parent will get very irritated.

'Andrew, will you empty the litter box?'
'Yeah, sure. In a little while, okay?'
'Andrew, you said you were going to take out the litter box.'
'Yeah, Mum, I will. Don't worry.'
'When?'
'I will. Soon.'

'Andrew, I asked you to take out the litter box earlier this afternoon, and I have kept reminding you. I am sick and tired of always having to tell you to do things. You should do it without always having to be asked.'
'I'm sorry, Mum. I forgot.'
'You forgot? You forgot? When are you going to grow up?'

A better way:

'Andrew, will you empty the litter box?'
'Yeah, sure. In a little while, okay?'
'No. Do it now.'
'I will, in a while.'
'No. Now!'
'No. I'm in the middle of doing something. Besides, you don't have to yell.'

'Andrew! Now!'
'All right. But you don't have to always yell at me.'

It is the only way.

'If she won't do for me ...'

With the contemporary teenager chores may not get done, at least not without a hassle. And in response, parents do get angry and, not unjustifiably, may feel taken advantage of. 'She is going to have to do her chores without my nagging her all of the time – or she's going to be sorry. I'll take things away. Privileges. Or maybe I just won't do anything for her. She won't do what I want. I won't do what she wants. Next time Natalie wants a lift somewhere, let's see what happens. That would teach her that the world is not just give, give, give.'

There is an important line here. Let us say that a child has just done something that really makes his mother angry. She was trying to tidy up the living room, asked for his help, and all he did was to give her a hard time, refusing to lift a finger. As a result, she is annoyed with him. If he then asks for a lift into town – not something which had been previously planned – whereas she might have said yes, on this occasion she is sufficiently irritated with him not to want to do him a favour. And so the answer is no. This seems fine.

The lesson learned is a reasonable one. She is not

prepared to put herself out and take him to the shops as a consequence of his being a lazy slob. He can jolly well get the bus. Acting like a lazy slob does make people, in particular his mother, angry. And when you make people angry, they are not going to feel as disposed to do you favours as they might otherwise have done.

But, on the other hand, let us say a teenage child is regularly lazy and unhelpful. Should the parent try to institute a more general campaign?

So long as you continue to act like a lazy slob around the house, I am not going to do any favours for you.

That is, I will not take him to friends' houses or to skating rinks. I will not give him a fiver for snacks after an outing to the cinema. I will not do any of the little extra things that parents do for their children.

That line of action has a very different message from the more simple 'I am at this particular moment too annoyed at you to feel like giving you a lift to the shops.' And many parents for very good reasons would not want to pursue this much tougher course.

The underlying question is: What is the role of the parent? Should parents be on the same level as their children or not?

Parents need to be above children – protectors, guides and nurturers. On the one hand, this means that parents are the bosses because they are the parents – not because they do not make mistakes. Yet alongside this greater authority they also – in many cases – offer the unconditional deal: I give to you what I feel are the basic rights of any child which definitely include favours done purely for your benefit. I do this regardless of what you do. Your behaviour and what I believe are your basic rights as a child are not tied together.

But many parents feel performance and privileges should be invariably linked. And many professionals in child psychology would support this view. If teenagers don't co-operate around the house, then parents should not do any of the extras for them. This is not an unreasonable approach. It is harsher than the unconditional deal.

What does the unconditional deal teach? Maybe only that there are suckers in the world who can be taken advantage of, treated like dirt, and still they will be nice to you. But maybe it teaches something altogether different. Maybe it teaches that – in a world so governed by money and exchange relationships – there are ways of relating between humans that transcend the notion 'I'll do for you if you'll do for me.' Maybe it teaches that out of love and commitment people give to others without guarantees of return. And maybe being on the receiving end of such a deal creates a person who is willing to act the same with others.

As for chores around the house, it is the case that if children are expected to do them, and if parents keep on at their children to do what they are supposed to do, expressing displeasure when they do not, the chores will get done, more or less. But there is no getting around the fact that with the new teenager it can be very wearing.

The consolation prize

With most teenagers, parents do have to expend an enormous amount of energy in order to produce a small amount of teenage labour. At times the effort/reward ratio hardly seems worth it, but ultimately things are not as futile as they may seem.

It was always Nick's job to bring in the wheelie bin from the street when he got home from school on Wednesday afternoons. But, without fail, when his father got home from work on Wednesdays the wheelie bin was still out in the street. Nick would then be asked to go out and bring it in. And then one day, soon after he had started in the sixth form, his father came home and the wheelie bin was not still standing out in the street. And from that day onwards, more or less without exception, Nick did bring in the bin when he got home from school. Why? Had something happened that finally convinced Nick that he should bring in the wheelie bin? Or had the repeated lesson finally sunk in by sheer accumulated weight? It was probably neither explanation. Nick had matured, plain and simple. For all those years Nick knew what he should do but just did not feel like doing it. The idea in his budding conscience was just not strong enough to counteract the immediate wants. As Nick matured he finally got to the point where the voice of responsibility did prevail over the need for immediate gratification. And from then on the responsibility always won out. It gradually became a habit.

Family hassles

Before going on to issues that move into the external world, there are still some issues concerning the home, though not strictly between parent and teenager, that are worth discussion.

Sibling rivalry

Sixteen-year-old Caroline to her 14-year-old sister Rachel:

> *'Rachel, you took my white jumper.'*
> *'I did not.'* [Actually she did.]
> *'Oh yes you did. Don't you lie. I want it back.'*
> *'I don't have it. Now get out of my room.'*
> *'Rachel, you're such a liar.'*

Instead of leaving, Caroline begins to go through her sister's chest of drawers.

> *'Stop that! Get out of my room!'*

Caroline ignores her, whereupon Rachel tries to pull her sister away from the dressing table. Caroline, who is bigger and stronger, pushes her away.

'Get the fuck off me!'

Rachel picks up a hairbrush and hits her sister rather hard on the back with it. 'You little bitch,' says Caroline as she turns and punches Rachel with all of her strength, hitting her in the stomach and almost knocking the wind out of her. Rachel, crying and screaming, runs from the room. Caroline runs in pursuit. Their mother, who was reading in the living room, looks up to see her two daughters rush into the room.

'Caroline's crazy. She attacked me. She should be in a mental hospital.'
'I can't stand her, Mum. She is always taking my stuff!'
'I didn't take anything. She comes in my room, and goes through my drawers, and I can't get her out, and then she hits me in the stomach as hard as she can. I think she injured my intestine. Also she said "Fuck" at me.'
'She hit me with a brush. I swear to God, Mum, one of these days I'm going to kill her unless you do something about her. I mean it, Mum.'
'See, Mum, she said she's going to kill me. She's crazy.'

'No, you're both wrong,' [said the girls' mother]. *'I am going to kill both of you. Now.'*

Teenagers are bigger and stronger than they were as young children. Sibling rivalry can take on new levels of violence. Brothers and sisters can and do injure each other. Usually their fights do not go that far, but when they threaten to, parents must intervene. The message must be: 'You may not do anything that could cause injury to your sister. And I will do anything to make sure that that does not happen.' And parents should not hold back from calling the police if a situation goes beyond what they can handle. The message must be that risk of injury will not be allowed.

Yet the general rules for battling siblings remain the same as when they were younger. The only useful intervention by parents is to separate and banish, particularly if there is an overwhelming physical danger. Other than doing this, parents intervene in sibling battles at their peril.

Brothers and sisters will always fight with each other. It is what they do. Families can have territorial ground rules to cover such issues as computer use, bathroom use, clothes, etc. Such rules are good. But they will not prevent fighting. Nothing will do that.

Parental intervention is always problematic, because as soon as parents intervene in a sibling battle the nature of that battle totally changes. No matter what the initial issue was, suddenly it becomes a contest for parental favour. The combatants no longer have any interest in resolving the problem. Now all they care about is getting their parent on their side.

> *'All right. I want each of you to tell me, one at a time, what happened.'*

This request ranks right up with the famous political phrase 'Crisis, what crisis?' as words that guarantee disaster.

> *'Mum, nothing of mine is safe from her. She takes anything, and she ruins my clothes.'*
> *'I only did it once. Her stupid pashmina. And it wasn't even my fault, and she never forgets it.'*
> *'Oh? And what about my green top? And my hair ties?'*
> *'You're the liar. The hair tie was already broken.'*

They will go on forever. And not only will a parent taking on the role of judge promote endless case pleading, but such a role colours the relationship between the two siblings. Older will now usually hate younger, because younger can more commonly enlist parent as a protector. It just doesn't work out when parents try to play the role of Solomon in their children's battles with each other. It really is better to leave them alone to work out their own disagreements:

'I'm really not interested in what the problem is. You two are just going to somehow have to sort it out on your own.'
'But, Mum, that's not fair. You don't understand what she gets away with.'
'I really don't want to hear about it.'

If parents stay out of the way, siblings really can resolve the majority of their disputes. They will do so in their own way, probably not without squabbling and often not exactly as their parents would have wanted. Assuming there's no threat of serious physical violence, the absence of parents facilitates this resolution.

Parent against parent

The additional complications of broken families and step-parenting are discussed later on, but even in a situation where a child is living with its two natural parents there is plenty of scope for creating divisions. Many adolescents are adept at making trouble between their parents by playing them off against each other.

'Mum, could you give me a lift to Lucy's house? Her mother can bring me home. I'll be home by 9 o'clock. I promise.'
'No, Melissa. It's a school night and you have homework to do.'
'But, Mum, I just have a little homework and I can do it after I get back.'

'No, Melissa. And that's final.'
'Mummy.'

Thirty minutes later:

'Donald, where's Melissa? She's been awfully quiet.'
'What do you mean? I drove her over to Lucy's house half an hour ago.'
'You did what?'
'Yeah, she asked me to. She said you'd said it was okay but you were too busy to take her.'
'Why, that little shit! I said nothing of the sort. Why didn't you ask me?'
'Why should I? I thought you said it was all right.'
'You should have checked with me. You know how devious she is. Besides, she's not allowed out on school nights.'
'I didn't know that was a rule.'
'You don't know anything because you don't pay any attention to anything that's going on with her. You leave everything for me to handle. You just sit here in your chair and watch the news.'
'Don't you start with me, Marion.'
'I'll start on whatever I please.'

When teenage children cause trouble, the trouble they cause often does not remain focused only on them.

It is a fact that when raising children parents are not

always united. Hence they become vulnerable to disagreements arising between them for every problem created by their children. And teenage children often make it more difficult by taking advantage of parental disagreements whenever they can.

In order to cope with this kind of thing parents have to know their own child. If a teenager has bent (or broken) the truth in the past about what one or the other parent said, then it is a good idea for the parents to check with each other.

'Marion, did you say it was okay for Melissa to go over to Lucy's house?'
'I certainly did not. What's she been saying?'

But there are situations where it is not always convenient or possible to have each parent check with the other:

I asked Mum before she left for her meeting if it was okay for me to go over to Lucy's house, and she said yes. Could you give me a lift over there?

Melissa knows she will be home before her mother's return from her meeting, and is gambling that the visit to Lucy's house will not be mentioned by her father.

Often they get away with this deception, undetected. But what if they are caught after the fact?

'How was your meeting?'
'Pretty good, but Kathleen Thompson certainly can be
long-winded. Anything happen here?'
'No. Melissa is back from Lucy's and your sister
called, but said she would ring you in the morning.'
'Melissa is back from where?'

At this point Melissa should be confronted with her deviousness.

'You told me that your mother said that it was okay for
you to go to Lucy's. You lied to me.'

Beyond confronting Melissa with her lie and letting her know that they don't like it, there is little more that parents can or should do. Of course, you can more severely reprimand or punish a teenager for deviousness, but you will have virtually no effect whatsoever. For such teenagers the bottom line is always whether they think they can get away with it. If in any given instance they believe they can, they'll try, and what happened after they were caught last week will not deter them this week.

Sometimes deviousness works for them. Parents must try to have good communication in order to keep ahead of the game, but that is not always possible. And if children do occasionally succeed in outwitting their parents, it's no big disaster.

'She tricked us.'
'Yes, I suppose she did.'

Each parent in charge of their own scene

But it is not always adolescent deviousness that pits parent against parent. They can often disagree themselves. And what will always set off a serious battle is the intrusion of one parent on a scene already in progress.

Sean's mother came into his room:

'Sean, I thought I told you to turn down your stereo.'
'I did.'
'It's just as loud as it was.'
'It isn't. Anyway, this is the way I like it.'
'Sean, turn it down.'
'But I already did.'
'Sean, turn it down, or I'll turn it down.'
'Leave my stereo alone. I bought it with my own money.'
'Don't you dare tell me what or what not to do.'
'You can't touch my stereo.'
'You better watch it, Sean!'

Enter Sean's father, who was in the next room.

'You two are making more noise than his stereo. Elizabeth, it's not on that loud. Sean, just keep your door closed.'

'The stereo is too loud. I'm handling this.'
'You weren't handling it. You were just arguing. You
have to learn to back off sometimes, Elizabeth. You
and Sean always end up yelling at each other. It's like
two kids.'
'Don't you dare contradict me in front of Sean. Don't
you see what you're doing? You're giving him
permission to walk all over me. He knows you'll
always side with him.'
'You're wrong, Elizabeth. You don't know what it's
like. The two of you always screaming at each other.'

There is a cardinal rule. The rule is that once a parent
is involved in disciplining a child, the other parent
should stay out of it – except to back them up, or unless
invited to take over. They should never intervene if it is
to contradict, even if they totally disagree with what the
other parent is doing. To do so is a major mistake.
Intervention that contradicts has several consequences:

(i)   it undermines the authority of the first
       parent. There is no way around it. It says to
       the child, 'Your mother's authority is not
       absolute. You can count on me stepping in,
       if I don't like what she is doing', which in
       turn

(ii)   sabotages the son and mother in working
       things out (just as with siblings), because the

son always knows if he can keep the fight
going long enough his father will intervene
and

(iii) just as with siblings, it creates an unnecessary
source of anger – mother towards son. She
now has an ongoing grudge against her son,
because he can bring his father in on his side
against her. Last, and definitely worst of all,

(iv) it will invariably infuriate the first parent. He
or she will feel belittled ('I'm not a good
enough parent') and intruded upon ('This is
none of his business. It was between Sean
and me'). And serious and ongoing hostility
can result.

It is to be avoided. 'But isn't it better to prevent something from happening between the two of them? You should see how they go for each other sometimes.' Short of violence, where intervention is absolutely required – if necessary by calling the police – intervening will improve nothing. It will only make the intruded-upon parent more angry. 'But there can be real abuse, without its being physical.' This is true. Continual verbal abuse from parent to child can be damaging.

Jamie, you're an arsehole. You don't have any fucking sense. You're a loser and you always will be a loser.'

If the verbal abuse by one spouse is continual, and if attempts to stop it go unheeded, only then does it become appropriate to say something to Jamie. Then a parent does need to say that what the other parent is doing is bad, that it is that parent, not Jamie, who is at fault.

'Your father is wrong to say all those things to you. He gets too upset, and ends up saying things he shouldn't say.'

Although it is important to point this out to children who are the victims of repeated verbal abuse, it must be done with great caution nonetheless. Criticising another parent does set up an always unfortunate bond – in this instance, mother and son against father. If this is necessary in order to preserve a child's self-respect, then it has to happen, but it should never be done lightly.

In matters of child-rearing, parents like to feel backed up by their partner. This is very basic to marriages and it is something that single parents often cite as an extra burden. Dealing alone with a teenager without the support and relief of the other parent can be a lonely and wearing task. Husbands and wives want recognition for doing the best they can. They know that they make mistakes. Lots of them. They need support, not criticism. We would all like to point out what we perceive as our partner's mistakes, and what better time than when they are making them. But that just is not our best role. Ours is to support. Even comments made later in private should be delivered with caution.

> *I wish you would ease up in dealing with Susan. You should hear yourself sometimes. It really would be better if sometimes you could just let some things go. Even if they bother you.*

This sounds reasonable, but the fact is that many parents resent being told how to parent by their spouse. They can read it in an article, hear it on television, even hear it from a counsellor, but not from a spouse. (Friends and other family members should definitely be wary about criticising a child-raising practice without being asked. Often it can be tantamount to poking cobras with sticks.) Parents can, of course, discuss things after the fact, even criticise each other, but they should tread carefully.

Different parents, different rules

> *But we end up with different rules. Robert and Becca know that when it's just their father, he's going to say yes to lots of things that I wouldn't. Isn't it important that we be consistent?*

Not really. Parents can never expect that they will react

the same in all situations. They cannot communicate about everything and usually one parent is less strict than the other. There is nothing chiselled in stone that says parents must be the same in every situation. Children learn early that different rules apply in different circumstances — at home, at school, alone with friends — and they adapt their behaviour to each situation. In the same way they adapt to dealing with their mother and father.

> *If I need money I always ask Mum, because with Dad*
> *I always get less money and a lecture too.*

This is neither bad nor good. It is reality. What does have to be consistent is that when one parent is in charge, he or she is the boss and his or her rules apply.

PART THREE

*Reality and the
World Outside*

In this book so far we have looked at cosy subjects like rude, ungrateful teenagers, unwashed dishes and broken curfews. But there is a big world lying in wait out there – real, frightening, and very much a part of the lives of our teenage children. This is the adult world in which they will have to make their way for the rest of their lives – the world that includes sex, drugs, drinking, broken relationships and marriages. These and a thousand other hazards bring down adults with regularity; it is not surprising that they snare a good proportion of the semi-adults we call adolescents.

We have already seen how different the world that today's teenagers live in is from the one their parents inhabited. There is less deference, teenagers are more outspoken and they have all kinds of material expectations that did not used to exist. Yet there are other ways in which the world has changed. The pace of life and the rate of change continues to speed up. We also undoubtedly live in a more insecure and uncertain world. Terrorist attacks, security threats, rocketing divorce rates and worries about climate change all feed into a world which is less predictable and certain than just a generation ago. Adults tend to have a more global response to these kinds of worries. We count on our overall fabric of security to insulate us day to day and to make us feel more or less protected. But events over recent years have often threatened that fabric, leaving us feeling more vulnerable, our sense of security weakened by a pervasive unease.

The effect upon most children and teenagers tends to be different. Children worry about national disasters, but they are far more concerned about the immediate impact on their own personal lives. If events like terrorist attacks don't affect them personally, they seem not to worry, at least not nearly as much as we do. Unlike us, they deal with problems one by one. The global sense of unease we get from listening to alarming news is unfamiliar to them. Children's overall sense of security has a different base from ours. They automatically feel one degree separated from the world out there. So long as children are not out on their own, adults still protect them from the world as reported in news bulletins. No matter what happens, they know that they will probably go on living in the same house with the same parents, going to the same school. Their concerns will not change: Will Robbie ask me out? Will I pass my AS levels? Will I make a reasonable living? Will I be a loser like Uncle John? They are also aided by the world's continuing reassurances that life goes on.

But the domain of adults has become different and in many ways more problematic. What can we as parents do to help teenagers grow up and thrive in it?

We should largely do the same as we have always done. We cannot shield them from the adult world, nor should we lament how difficult it is for them to grow up and live in it. That is missing the point. We don't have to grieve for them. Because what children can do, better than we can, is adapt. The adult world that they will join may be full of dangers and challenges, but they will form their lives around that – around the bad and the good. Just as the technology that we still feel bewildered by is second nature to them. To them the world is not tragic; it is all they know. How will they be able to go out and live lives in this world with all its uncertainty? They can and they will.

What should we as parents do to best ensure that our children will live happy and full lives? How do you produce children who have confidence in themselves and a capacity to cope with the world they live in? The same as always. Give them a good core of nurturing but also keep making demands on them and make sure they always face up to the important challenges in their daily lives.

7

Divorce

Children do not like their parents to get divorced. But divorces happen anyway. Many divorces. It is a much-quoted fact that the current rate of divorce in Britain at over one in three marriages is one of the highest in Western Europe. Although there has recently been a slight decline in the number of divorces, this is principally because fewer people are getting married. Moreover, the official divorce figures do not take account of the break-ups of common law partnerships. Contemporary divorce rates are still six times higher than in the 1950s, even though there are now fewer marriages.

Divorces and family break-ups do create problems for children. That is inevitable. Most children learn to cope with divorce, but it is always a problem for them.

Are children inevitably scarred by divorce? Opinions vary (and this is a hotly contested political area), but, at the very least, divorce is a major disruption in their lives.

'I want to worry about acne, not this.'

Couldn't they at least have waited until I had finished school? I don't want to have to deal with this.

There is no good time in the life of a child for his or her parents to divorce. For each age divorce creates its own special problems. Adolescence is the period in which children don't even want to think about their parents. They want distance. They also want stability. No major disruptions, please, beyond the battles that the teenager initiates.

Divorce destroys this equilibrium.

Yeah. I want to be able to spend my time worrying about adolescent things like sex, my friends and school. And now I can't even deal with that because I keep worrying about Mum and Dad. It's shitty.

Children genuinely resent their parents for putting their own adult needs and problems before theirs.

So what, she's put up with him for seventeen years. What's her big hurry that she can't wait a couple more?

One's parents divorcing is a major loss for teenagers. Teenagers want separation but on their own terms. The loss of the safety and security provided by the nuclear family is not what they have in mind.

Moving

A major problem for adolescents, one that does not trouble pre-teens nearly as much, is that divorce often leads to a change of residence.

I'm not going to leave my friends. Mum says she can't afford to keep the house now, and she's looking at houses in Ashton, which she says are cheaper. But I'm not moving there. No way. I don't know anybody who goes to Ashton Comprehensive. And I don't think I'd fit in there so well.

A sudden move can be difficult for a teenager during secondary school, when friendships are paramount. It will cause deep resentment for even the mature and understanding adolescent. Plans that at least allow the teenager to carry on at the same school are often worth some inconvenience to the parents. But sometimes this accommodation is not possible. And where not, such a move can be hard for teenagers.

While a move may be unavoidable, certain other, very negative aspects of divorce are not so inevitable. Here the parents' behaviour is critical in how seriously the divorce will ultimately affect their children.

'It was my fault.'
If I weren't being so difficult and giving them so much
trouble, then I don't think they would have got
divorced. Most of the time when they were fighting, it
had to do with me. I know the divorce was my fault.

Unfortunately, children do quite frequently feel that they have caused their parents' divorce. More often than not, there really is not much real basis for that feeling, but it's there anyway. This misconception can bring on a crushing amount of guilt. For this reason it probably is a good idea for at least one parent to address the subject with their children, even if they haven't said a word about it.

Evan, do you think it was in any way your fault that
your mother and I separated?

And even if he says 'No', parents should still respond:

I just wanted you to know that though you have upset
us at times, and your mother and I did have fights
about you, you are not the reason we separated. That
had to do with us. Things had been going wrong
between us for a long time that had nothing to do with
you.

Even explanations as simple as this really can help. To hear it directly, from the horse's mouth, can allay many concerns. And a parent need not go into great depth either.

> 'Your mother really began to treat me too much like a child. And over the last couple of years it made me have trouble getting an erection when we had sex. I'm vulnerable to depressive episodes, and your mother would get hostile when I would get depressed.'
> 'Dad! Please!'

They don't want to hear about it. Simple, straightforward, and without a lot of details is all they want or need to hear about the reasons for a separation.

Caught in between

Probably the most distressing of all divorce situations is for teenagers to feel caught in the middle. The main rule for parents getting a divorce is not to pull their children into the battle, not in any way, shape or form. Never do it.

> I am not saying this because I want you to think any worse of your father. I really mean that. It is only that I want you to get a proper understanding of what went on. I just don't want you to think badly of me. But your father was never an easy man to care about. He can be

very cold. You know that. He has this way of making it seem that everything was always my fault. You know how he does the same thing with you and Mark.

I am not prying. But I do think that I have the right to know if your mother and Tom say anything about me. That is my business.

It may be hard for parents to resist these ploys, but they must. It is simply not fair to children to ask them to take sides. It is not fair to involve them in any adult conflict, much less one between their parents. They cannot handle it. It's bad for them.

As already stated, the main psychological work of adolescence is that teenagers pull away from their parents in order to establish a necessary sense of their own independence. To pull them back into the web of their parents' divorce can destroy that process. Worse still, it can stir up inappropriate feelings towards one parent or the other as parents invite them into an adult complicity, even an intimacy, that is far too adult for adolescents to understand and handle. Once these feelings are stirred up they lead only to unpleasant results, and create intolerable conflicts within the teenager.

It may be hard for parents to avoid pulling their children into the divorce, even unintentionally. It can be particularly hard when one parent hears from the children that the other parent is not playing by the rules.

Dad said that one of the reasons that you got divorced was because you had no sense of money, which is also why you keep running short now, not because he does not give you enough maintenance.

This cries out for a response.

I mean, I do have to put Sam right. Am I just supposed to let his father say anything? I know him. He'll convince them that I was the worst bitch in the world and he was a saint.

Blatant untruths deserve simple rebuttals. But beyond that, the great urge to 'set the record straight' should be resisted. There is a hidden benefit to this strategy. In time, in the majority of instances, it is the parent who refrained from speaking ill of the other, who did not try to bring the children to his or her 'side', who comes out looking the best.

Mum always said all this stuff about Dad, and I never knew what to think. But Dad always stayed out of it. I never liked it when Mum said all that stuff. I suppose she had her difficulties.

When one parent puts his or her own needs (usually, to get back at the divorced spouse) over their children's needs, adolescents are perceptive enough to see the gambit for what it really is. We may not understand, but our children do not really care who was to blame. Remember, adolescents in particular are mainly (and obsessively) interested in themselves. Nor is it important that they 'know the truth'. Only to us is it important, not to them. They just want to know that their parents are okay and that their parents still love them. Maybe someday they will want to know, when they can deal with it as adults, and at a distance. But not now.

We owe it to our children not to enmesh them in our adult affairs. As much as we can, we should try to provide them with a childhood, with an adolescence. This is where they grow best.

Parenting alone

There are an estimated 1.9 million lone-parent families in Britain today – a figure which has seen a steady and continuing increase. Over three million children – around one in four – are being brought up in a single-parent home. In 90 per cent of cases this is the mother.

Raising a child alone is usually a more difficult task than doing it with a partner. In many ways, the difficulties in single-parent homes are more for the parents than for their children.

Certainly it is to a child's advantage to have both parents in the home, but children can adapt to many kinds of living arrangements, and they tend to flourish according to how the parenting is done, rather than whether there are two married parents in the home or not.

Probably the greatest difficulty for the single parent of a teenager is that there is no one to fall back on – either for day-to-day relief during shrieking battles or for support when difficult decisions must be made. Parenting jointly brings occasional relief.

> *'Jessica, have you taken leave of your senses? Didn't you realise what you were doing?'*
> *'I'll do whatever I like, and I won't listen to anything you or Dad says.'*
> *'I can't deal with her any more, Edward. You try.'*
> *'Just like your mother says, you must not have a brain in your head. Do you know what could happen to you?'*

Some single parents are lucky enough to have some kind of burden-sharing arrangement with the other parent who now lives elsewhere but fairly close by. Some live with relatives. But many must do it all on their own.

Though single parents are perfectly capable of raising teenagers, having to parent alone is hard. Yet though alone, single parents do not have to be completely alone.

They can seek out support. Talking with friends, relatives, the woman next to you in the GP's waiting room who is glancing at the book on adolescence, anybody really, can be useful. They cannot help with the work, they cannot be there at the moments of decision, but talking with others – who have experience or who are facing similar quandaries – is virtually a necessity. It is a mistake to be a parent in isolation.

> *Ellen, it was unbelievable. I was sitting at home thinking that Lisa was at her friend Karen's revising, and then she calls and asks me to pick her up at Megan Shaw's, who I had said she was absolutely not allowed to hang around with. Lisa thinks I say stuff and it doesn't mean anything, so I really let her have it when I picked her up. I don't know what I'm going to do with her.*

Ellen does not have any solutions but she does fulfil the very important task of making you feel not quite so alone.

Step-parenting

Alas, not all cases of blended families end up living the happy scenarios depicted in the American TV sit-com *The Brady Bunch*.

> *'You can't tell me what to do, you're not my father.'*

'It's not just that he won't obey his step-father. I can't believe how disrespectful he is to him sometimes. And not just Chris, Sarah does it too. Both of them. They actually ignore him, they act as if he isn't talking. They are impossibly rude to him.'

'Yeah, well, he's an asshole. I don't know why Mum married him. I guess she was lonely.'

'And it's not that I compare him to Dad. It's that he really is an asshole. Even the way he talks. "Marian, when shall we leave?" What an asshole! It's better that I ignore him instead of punching him in his fucking face.'

'And he always has his hands all over her. He's disgusting. He's such a lech. And I can't believe her. She likes it. It makes me cringe. I feel like I don't know her.'

'And you should see how he holds his fork.'

'They don't give him a chance. He's really a much nicer man than their father.'

'Don't you think you should at least try to get along with him? At least for my sake?'

'See. She always says that. She could have waited to

get married. What's her hurry? She sure didn't consult
me about whether they should get married.'
'That's not true. I asked you about it.'
'Sure. What am I supposed to say, "No, Mum, don't
marry him"? She should have known.'

And it is not only with step-fathers. Teenagers can be
equally nasty to step-mothers, even though they are less
likely to be living with them full-time.

'You're going to have to obey your step-mother.'
'But, Dad, she's a lunatic about tidying up. I put
something down for a second and she's after me. It
wasn't this way before she came in the house. It's not
fair to me. Why should I have to change after all these
years? I didn't marry her.'

Step-parents are not impervious to this abuse by their
step-children.

'I hate him. He's trying to ruin our marriage and he's
doing a very good job.'
'Now, Elaine, you have to understand. Timmy's not
a bad kid. It is a big change. We're asking him to
change a lot, and maybe it's not reasonable to want
him to be quite what you're used to.'
'He just wraps you around his little finger. You should
hear what he says to me when you're not around. He

204

*doesn't do anything and he thinks he can treat me like
a servant. I don't think you really know what kind of
a child you've brought up. He says anything to you
and you believe him. Maybe I'm really the intruder.
Maybe I should just leave you two alone and go
away.'*

If the children are very young, a new step-parent in
the home can, over time, develop into the role of a true
parent. Some children live from an early age with a
mother and a step-father, but see their natural father
with regularity. (Less often, they're living with their
natural father and see their mother outside the home.)
These children see themselves as having two fathers,
usually with a stronger attachment to the step-father.
They do not feel any conflict about having 'two
fathers'. To them it seems natural. In these situations
divided-loyalty problems are created by adults.

But if the children are older when the step-parent
appears on the scene, more usually they will not view
this new adult as a full, true parent. Often they will see
the step-parent as an intruder – in a home situation that
was already established – even as an intruder who perhaps caused or certainly ensured the permanent break-
up of the natural parents and who now competes for the
attention of the true parent. The many reasons for
resenting a step-parent are normal and understandable.
Add to that a teenager's normal wish not to do any-

thing, add the knack for making excuses and acting like a sullen lazy slob, and you have a problem. It is small wonder that second marriages, which entail a re-ordered family, are more fragile and likely to fall apart than first marriages.

Many teenage step-children, acting obnoxiously under these circumstances, genuinely believe that they are doing nothing wrong. With a divorce and remar-riage, they feel that their parents' original contract with them has been broken and that now, in all fairness, they are free to act as they wish. It has always been their home. The step-parent is but an invader on their terri-tory – with no right to tell them what to do. Their deal never included a new parent. It was not their choice. They feel short-changed. They may be right. Yet though it may not be what they wanted, it is what they have got. And they must live with it.

'Must I like my step-son?'

Just like in fairy tales, real step-children often genuinely do not like a step-parent, and real step-parents often genuinely do not like their step-children, especially when those step-children consistently give them a hard time.

I wanted it to go well. I wanted to be a nice parent. I did try. But I feel so rejected. They treat me like dirt. What did I ever do to deserve this? You know how I

really feel about the two of them? I think they're
spoiled brats.

Fortunately, it is not necessary for step-parent and step-child to like each other. It would be nice if it happened, but it does not have to be. What is necessary is that the facts of the situation – a step-child's unpleasant behaviour or a step-parent's difficult personality – must be given recognition by the arbiter, the natural parent.

I know that Stephen gives you a hard time. I've done
all that I can think of to get him to behave better, and I
know that it hasn't worked. He is awful to you, and
I'm sorry about that. I only hope it doesn't spoil things
between the two of us.

It is always a mistake to downplay how obnoxious, how disrespectful a step-child might be. And even though there may be nothing one can do about it, just recognising how bad it is can go a long way towards making an abused step-parent feel not quite so abused.

Likewise with children and difficult step-parents:

I know Vivienne gets very upset sometimes when you
don't tidy up after yourself, and I know that compared
to plenty of children you're really not that bad about
cleaning up. But that's the way she is. And I do
understand that her standards of tidiness can get to you

sometimes. Nobody says you have to like her. But I do want you to treat her with respect.

One big happy family it is not. But it can work out anyway.

8

School

School performance goes a long way towards shaping an adolescent's future. Many parents view their teenager's school reports as the first true indication of whether they will be successful in life. But parents of teenagers must remember that they serve much the same purpose as the trainer of a fighter: he can train his man but cannot go into the ring with him. The best you can do is give advice between rounds.

You have to spend more time on your homework. It's your future that's at stake. You don't want to end up like your uncle Leo, do you?

A D? You got a D in your Spanish test? How? I

thought you said you revised properly, that you knew the chapter.

You have detention all next week? ... You did what during assembly?

It can be frustrating. Parents have little direct control over how their teenagers do in school.

Academic performance

However, parents do have considerable *influence* over their children's school performance. But, for the most part, even influence is restricted to the primary school years. Parents who help their children in school start early. They put time, energy and caring into school-related activities. They read to and with their children. They show a continuing interest in schoolwork. When there's homework they make sure that their children do it, and make clear that it is a top priority. By their attitude, their interest and their willingness to participate, they communicate that school is very important.

Eleven-year-olds with a positive attitude towards school and good work habits normally become 16-year-olds with a positive attitude towards school and good work habits. Conversely, 11-year-olds who hate schoolwork and have never been able to sit down and do homework on their own are almost always going to have a rough time in secondary school. Children are the product of all that has gone on before. Parents who hope to bring about major changes in an adolescent's school performance are quite likely to be disappointed. This does not mean that parents should not try. But they do need to be aware that much has already been established. Of course, maddeningly, previously good students may switch off and do poorly in secondary school. Usually, but not always, this is because they discover and are overwhelmed by the joys of socialising or because something is going wrong in other parts of their life.

What parents can do

A combination of ambition and anxiety is what motivates adolescents to do their schoolwork. The anxiety is very important. (It works well with adults too.) The anxiety is the fear of what will happen if they do not do their schoolwork. Their parents will be angry with them and they want to avoid unnecessary battles. They may lose privileges. However, their main fear is that failure can jeopardise their future. This is a powerful motivator. But some teenagers can completely shut out even this warning siren.

> *'You really don't worry about your future?'*
> *'Occasionally I do ... But no, otherwise I don't think about it.'*

Without anxiety as a regular prod, teenagers drift, force their worries away, and go nowhere.

But I'm not just going to sit still and watch my child waste their chances. There must be something I can do about it.

Parents do have options, of course. Those who can afford it send their children to boarding schools with a highly structured regime and an environment that promises to lick their children into shape. (Of course this is not to every parent's taste or bank balance.) Some children do respond positively to the usually greater structure of boarding schools. Some do not. For parents who cannot afford or do not choose such an option, what alternatives are there?

Motivating your teenager

There are a number of ways to motivate teenagers to do their schoolwork. One common practice is to use punishment.

If you do not get all Cs or better this term, we are going to ground you until your marks improve.

Similar motivators include withholding permission to drive, forbidding an upcoming trip, altering plans for a special summer holiday. Parents also use the promise of reward.

If you do really well in your AS levels we'll buy you a car.

Threats or promises do sometimes work, but more often than not they only work for a while. They rarely solve the problem.

Another common motivating technique is the motivational lecture.

Two years from now you will have left school and you're going to be on your own. It's up to you what's going to happen. If you do well enough you can go to university, and we will help you with that. But right now, you won't be able to go anywhere. All that you will be qualified for is to fry burgers, or stack shelves in a supermarket.

In some homes these lectures are given very frequently and are then often followed by even shorter, more passionate versions.

You do nothing. I can't stand watching you. You're going to end up a drop-out ... a pathetic drop-out.

Perhaps unfortunately, these types of intervention usually have little positive effect except that they may help the parent feel better, which is fine. They're not likely to help the student.

Here's the main problem with all these ploys: capable children who perform poorly in school do not lack the desire for success. Most of them do want to do well in school.

> *'Do you want to do better in school?'*
> *'Yeah.'*
> *'So why don't you?'*
> *'I don't know. I just never feel like doing the work. I*
> *say to myself sometimes that I'm going to start to try in*
> *school. But it never gets anywhere, because I never can*
> *get myself to do it. I don't know why I can't. I*
> *suppose I'm just lazy.'*

One might say that they are motivated but not disciplined. They would like to do better; they just cannot make themselves. The one motivator that might drive them along – anxiety about their future – is too successfully pushed away.

Therefore, working on motivation rarely produces results.

So what's left?

Supervision

There really is only one form of parental intervention with teenagers that can make a difference: direct supervision of their child's study. There are many ways to do this but it is never easy. One plan can involve a mutually accepted study time with at least one parent in the house and available for supervision. During study time the teenager is not allowed to do anything else. No TV. No phone calls. No texting and no Internet (except strictly for educational purposes). In other words, none of the multiple distractions usually available to the modern teenager. Nothing except schoolwork.

The study period must always be in force regardless of whether a child has homework or not. This last proviso is necessary because the study-time plan can quickly be defeated:

I don't have any homework.

I did it in school.

I wasn't there when they set the homework.

Or the ultimate:

I forgot my books at school.

Tough. The study period remains. During the study period the child is not allowed to do anything other than schoolwork. If that means staring into space for an hour, so be it. Parents cannot make a child do homework. But they can usually enforce that during a specified time period their child does nothing else.

It is a good idea to set up a study period of limited and specified duration. When the time is up, the teenager is free to do whatever he or she wants. This plan works best because it says to the student, 'If I can just survive until 9 o'clock, then no matter what, I'm free.'

It defeats the object if adolescents are allowed to lock themselves in their room during the study period. Parents need to check regularly. Sometimes working at a kitchen table, away from the distractions of one's room, can further the cause. Or working in another room with the door ajar. Listening to music is not necessarily ruled out. With some children, it can actually help them to get on with their work.

Important to the success of this plan is that parents must stay with it. Initial resistance may be fierce and the amount of work done limited. But over time, with parental persistence, some children can conform to study time. They will not fight it so much. They will like the fact that the work is now getting done, that they are getting fewer hassles from their teachers, and that their marks are improving.

Parents can check regularly to make sure that homework is done. This usually requires the co-operation of the school because the parents will need to know, for example through the homework diary, what has been set. Some teachers don't mind taking the time required to help in this regard, but others do.

One problem with supervision plans is that a great deal of parental time and effort is required. This is certainly the case when, as often happens, the student in question does not meekly accept the added supervision. Teenagers absolutely hate it. Particularly at first, they will fight it tooth and nail.

So supervision can be yet another thoroughly unpleasant task. And parents cannot give up. Just because a student has settled into a regular routine of study does not mean that the pattern will hold when supervision ceases. Almost certainly it will not.

Parental supervision should be looked on as a long-term job – two or even three years perhaps.

But if he is constantly supervised, if he only does his work with us standing over him, how will he ever learn to do it himself? Isn't it a necessary part of independence that they are allowed to fail, and then learning that they can fail, they'll start to work on their own?

If only that were true – just allow secondary school students to learn by their failures. But alas for the majority it does not work. They learn nothing. They only keep failing.

But if they go on to university, with no parents to stand over them, never having learned to work on their own, won't they just stop working and drop out?

Some do. But the point about the hands-on approach with failing students is that if they can be made to study regularly, over an extended period of time, then it usually becomes a habit. Having been able to study for significant periods of time, if they then choose to make themselves study, even without the overseer, they are more able to accept their new taskmaster – themselves.

With adolescents who, for whatever reason, cannot make themselves do their schoolwork, more supervision is the only real answer. Unfortunately, even this does not always work. There are some teenagers who resist even the best parental efforts. There are some who, despite all that may be done, continue to fail.

Time as an ally

Yet even with those who continue to fail despite every effort, all is still not lost. Waiting in the wings, ready to come on in the not too distant future, is one last, very powerful force: true independence. Shortly, they will be on their own and they know it. The anxiety they have held at bay these many years will finally catch up with them. And maybe they will have matured enough to be ready for it.

I know I completely messed about at school. I just played around the whole time. But now I will have to get my act together. I don't have a choice. Either I start getting serious and work at something, or I'm going to screw up my whole life. I really will end up as a drop-out.

Some former school failures go on to higher education later on. Some do well. Some perfectly successful adults were disasters at school. They did get their act together. On their own. When they had to.

What should parents do with teenage children who do badly in school and could do much better? If parents wish to put in the effort, if they are willing to put up with considerable unpleasantness, they can actively supervise their children's schoolwork at home. And this may help. But it may not. If not, their only recourse is to wait and to hope that with time, with maturity, with anxiety about the future looming not on the horizon but directly overhead, their children will at last develop some self-discipline and be willing and able to work.

Troublemakers in school

Academic performance is usually of first concern for most parents, but misbehaviour in school can be an accompanying and sometimes especially trying problem.

'Hello, Mrs Shepardson, this is the school office. We are calling just to check and make sure that you knew that Jordan was not in school today.'
'He wasn't?'

'This is just a routine call to let you know that Jordan was not in school today. Thank you.'

Click.

Hello, Mr Tellman, this is the deputy head calling. Did you get our note saying that Ellen was suspended for three days? She cannot come back to school until this Friday. At that time she will have to be accompanied by a parent.

Mrs Windsor, this is Margaret Smith from St Saviour's School. We just wanted you to know that Charlie did not show up for his detentions for the last two days, and since he has to do two for every one detention missed, he will now have to attend detention on four days running.

These situations seem to demand a parental response.

Jordan, you bunked off school today. You're grounded for two weeks.

Charlie, you've been missing detentions. Well, you can miss going out this weekend.

Yet it is far from clear that such responses are necessary or even desirable. How much do parents want to get involved with behaviour problems that take place in a realm that already has its own system for behaviour control? One such system at a time is probably enough. Parents should confront their children. They should certainly voice their displeasure.

> *I got a call today from your school. They said you have not been turning up for detention. I do not know what your problem is, and I really don't care. But you had better start doing those detentions. I do not want to get any more calls from the school.*

Beyond that, involvement may be counterproductive. Parents may ultimately be better off letting their teenage children deal on their own with the consequences of their behaviour in the outside world.

Parents should also be wary of listening too much to their children's side of the story.

> *Dad, it's just like I've been saying. Mr Farrow doesn't like me. I don't know why, but it's always me who's the one who gets in trouble in Chemistry. I swear to God, plenty of other people are doing more stuff than me and aren't getting in any trouble. He's really picking on me, Dad.*

Parents may be tempted to intervene, as they might have done in primary school, but they do so at their peril. It is far better simply to say, 'I don't know what the problem is. Maybe Mr Farrow is being unfair. But you're 16 years old and you ought to realise that in years to come you will have to deal with all sorts of difficult people as well as unfair situations. So you're just going to have to work out whatever it is you have to do not to incur his wrath and to stay out of trouble. You'll have to sort this out on your own.'

It's the same issue yet again: as they get older we have to let go. They are no longer answerable just to us. They become answerable to their school, to their employers, to the police, even to the state. Gradually, responsibility for their actions must and does leave our hands.

'Ronnie, I just got a call from the Inland Revenue. They say that you submitted fraudulent tax returns for the past three years. Well, son, you can just forget about going out on weekends for the next month.'
'But, Dad, Ros and I had planned to take the kids to the circus next weekend.'
'Well, son, you should have thought about that when you filed those dodgy tax returns.'
'Oh, Dad.'

9

The Electronic World

Competing for their attention

'Kate, can I talk to you?'

'In a minute.'

'No, now.'

'I can't, Mum. I'm talking to Elisha, Leanne, Sophia, Ben and Seth and I'm in the middle of doing my biology homework. And Hollyoaks has just started and you know that's my favourite programme.'

'Jeremy, can I speak to you for a minute?'

'No, Mum, not right now. I'm just in the middle of a shoot-out and if I stop now my man could be killed by the police and I'll lose a life.'

The electronic world has become, and will continue to

be, a huge presence in almost every home. Television, the telephone, the Internet, MP3 players, video games, games consoles – such widespread and varied sources of entertainment and information, and connection to peers, were simply unimaginable even in the quite recent past. As a result, if parents want something from a child once he or she reaches adolescence – time, help, even undivided attention – they are constantly up against stiff competition.

> *'Jessica, would you mind …'*
> *'Mum! Do I look like I can listen to you now? Please!'*

It often feels as if powerful magnetic waves are reaching out from the electronic devices and holding your child tightly. The iPod and the mobile phone are rather like their life-support systems, the child barely existing without being plugged in. And should you temporarily be able to separate them, the devices seem to exert a constant and powerful force, pulling the child back.

> *Helen, I got him! I got him! Hurry over with the list of chores.'*
> *'Dad, let go of my leg! Dad!'*
> *'Here are the chores.'*
> *'Oops, now I have lost him again.'*

It is a serious issue. The constant pull of TV, video games and electronic communication with friends makes it harder to accomplish what is supposed to go on in the home between parent and child: communication of basic information.

> *'I don't think I can pick you up tomorrow night from football practice, so you will have to take the bus home.'*
> *'What was that? Tell me later, I'm just in the middle of* Friends.*'*

Even the prospect of spending (quality) time together is more difficult. There are so many competing distractions.

> *'So. How is school going?'*
> *'Look, I can't talk now. OK. Please!'*
> *'But Daniel, I have a really good story about a time when your uncle Ralph and I went fishing that I know you have never heard before. It's so funny. I know you will like it.'*
> *'Yes, Dad, I'll listen. But I'm busy now. Tell me some other time.'*

Connection to peers

With the ever-increasing role of the electronic world in their lives, teenagers feel connected to a network of peers. Of course, in the not-so-recent past there was television (although comparatively fewer channels and only available during specified limited hours) and teenagers could always chat on their house phone. But aside from this, once the family was together at home there was not this permanent sense of connection to the world outside, especially through constant texting and web-surfing. Today it is as if the walls of the home are porous. Home is no longer a sanctuary from the wider world!

Despite all the concerns about Internet stalking and anonymous chat rooms, most Internet communication amongst teenagers is with others they already know — friends, or at least friends of friends — instant messaging or via the various social networking sites such as Bebo, MySpace or Facebook. These means of virtual communication have become a huge element in most teenagers' lives. Through the mass media too, especially TV shows, they also feel connected to other kids their age – some real, some fictitious. Teenagers today have access to a world of peers who constitute a vast source of norms and values separate from those they observe at home. Children have of course always used the line 'But everyone else's parents let them ...' However, today this kind of peer awareness reaches new possibilities.

> *'Alexander, please will you clean the bathroom?'*
> *'No way. Kids these days don't have to clean the bathroom.'*

'Well, I'm afraid that in this house they do, especially when they have been responsible for leaving it in such a mess.'

'But that's not right. It would make me the only kid in Britain who has to clean bathrooms.'

'Alexander, please clean the bathroom.'

'Wait a minute.' [Alexander runs off, sits down at the computer, and in sixty seconds is back.]

'No, you see, none of my friends' parents makes them clean bathrooms. I just checked on MSN. You can't ask me to clean the bathroom. It's not fair.'

Turning it off

What alternatives does a parent have? One option is to turn the device off or at least to set some limits.

Michaela's parents decided to disconnect their daughter from all access to the Internet.

'Omigod, what are you doing? You're killing me.'

'That is ridiculous, Michaela. We are not killing you.'

'You don't understand. Everyone will be talking about stuff and I won't have a clue what happened. I'll go to school and it will be like I've been on Mars.'

'That is ridiculous, Michaela.'

'No, it's not. And not only will I be more and more out of it, but there'll be this whole world that my friends have been part of that I won't have a clue about. I won't know about it and I will miss out on

the huge amount of time that my friends spend with
each other. You will be ripping the best, the biggest, the
most important piece of my life out of me.'

In truth, what would really happen? Michaela would probably miss out, given that online socialising is now such a big part of teenage life. But the teenage world is also rather like a soap opera. You can miss big scenes and still catch up with the underlying story.

'Jessie did it with Jack? I didn't know that.'
'Yeah, everyone knew about that.'
'I can't believe it. What did Laura think?'
'What do you think she thought? She was really pissed
off.'

The threat of being cut off will lead to familiar arguments for electronic access.

'But I need the Internet for my homework.'

'I need my video games. Life is so stressful at the
moment. Video games are my way of chilling out.
What is wrong with that?'

And there is some validity to their arguments. In an increasingly connected electronic world, being deprived of access makes things difficult. Parents will differ on how much time they are willing to let their children connect with it. But in many cases it is an idea to at least place some limits on total 'screen time'.

I'm really opposed to having my teenage son spend all his available time playing video games. I do not agree that my daughter has to be connected to her friends all of her waking moments. When I speak to my children, is it asking too much that I want them to answer?

They will fight you if you try to limit that time. They may not obey. But an option that all parents have if thcir teenagers do not abide by the limits they set is to temporarily remove electronic access and take away the PlayStation or Xbox. If children are unwilling to follow these rules, then they can – temporarily – have their access taken away. Internet access is not after all a God-given right.

Yes it is, idiot.

The best way of placing limits is to give the teenagers a choice about what they want to do. They can communicate with friends, play video games, etc., but it should not be *all* the time.

What will they do if they are not hooked up to a screen? They will have to find something else to do instead – that is the whole point.

Maybe they will even pester you.

'Dad, I am bored. Could you tell me that funny story about when you and Uncle Ralphie went fishing?'

Unlikely, perhaps.

But if parents want to have some control in the competition between them and the electronic world, they have to be willing – if necessary – to sometimes turn it off.

Parents can also have a helpful role in reminding – actually telling – their teenage child that all that goes on in the electronic world is not always real. In effect, you want to encourage a healthy scepticism about what they see and hear. Buying products is not necessarily going to make you more cool. And of course what people say and even who they say they are – especially on the Internet – is not always true. Teenagers know all of this, but it definitely does not hurt to remind them.

Unpleasant content

Probably what parents worry about the most is that the electronic world, in all its forms, contains material and contacts which parents do not want their children exposed to. Even though there are various forms of Internet parental controls, in a multi-channel world (where the content of many video games is also pretty unpleasant) all of this is increasingly difficult to police.

'You just don't know. There is so much sex and
violence. And the attitudes – everyone is so
disrespectful to everybody else. It's not surprising that
kids act the way they do. And with the Internet you
never know who is out there.'

There is indeed a great deal of sex and violence in the electronic media. Unfortunately it is often more immediately interesting to teenagers than content which does not include sex and violence. And some – not all – of what they see and hear portrays individuals acting towards others in very disrespectful, even degrading, ways, where the message is that this kind of behaviour is acceptable, even cool. There are still plenty of academic debates about the extent to which children are influenced by this kind of unpleasant content. Nevertheless, many parents feel instinctively that there should be limits.

How should one control access to this kind of nasty material? In addition to the various 'net nanny'-type programs, some parents prefer that their children access the Internet and play (especially online) games on a computer in a public room – the living room, a kitchen alcove – rather than in the seclusion of their bedroom. Even if parents cannot monitor everything that goes on, this can limit some of the more worrying access – although the spread of wireless networking in the home makes this kind of vigilance more difficult.

There is another powerful control against the undesirable influences of the electronic world. This control is how parents themselves act – towards their children, towards others. If I treat my children non-violently, with love, respect and consideration, and they see me acting that way towards others as well, such children will tend to act that way themselves. And they will tend to view much of what they see and hear in that context.

On the other hand, if I treat my children badly or they are raised in a moral vacuum, what they see and hear away from the home and their family will have a strong influence on them. They know nothing else. The effects of the electronic world will be far more influential.

10

Sex

Michael and Yvonne

'How old are you?'

'Fifteen.'

'Do you have a boyfriend?'

'Yeah. His name is Michael. Do you want to see a picture of him?'

'No, thanks. How old is Michael?'

'He's 16.'

'How long have you been going out with him?'

'This Thursday is going to be our four-month anniversary.'

'Do you love Michael?'

'Yeah, I love him a lot.'

'Does he love you?'

'Yes. And he tells me he does. He's not afraid to say it.'

'Do you and he have sex?'

'Yeah.'

'How often?'

'Maybe two, three times a week.'

'How do you get to do it that much?'

'Well, sometimes we meet after school at my house, when my parents aren't home. And sometimes on weekends, but I have to be in by 11 o'clock, and my parents are usually home.'

'Do you like having sex?'

'Yeah, of course I do.'

'Have you ever had an orgasm?'

'I'm not sure.'

'Why do you and Michael have sex as much as you do?'

'We like to.'

'Whose idea is it usually?'

'His. But I don't mind, really. I like to do it.'

'Do you use any kind of contraception?'

'Sometimes.'

'What do you mean, sometimes?'

'Well, sometimes Michael uses a condom.'

'Why not always?'

'Well, he doesn't like to use them. Sometimes he pulls out of me when he comes. And I know when I have my period, so I know when it's safe. But sometimes I guess we do take chances.'

'Don't you worry about STDs?'

'No, not really.'

'Have you ever thought of contraception for yourself?'

'Yeah. But I can't really talk to my parents. They'd have a fit if they knew I was having sex with Michael.'

'What if you got pregnant?'

'I don't know. I don't like to think about it. But I'd probably decide to have the baby. I wouldn't want to have an abortion. I think I would keep the baby.'

'What would Michael do?'

'I'm not that stupid. I know he probably wouldn't want to get married. Besides, we're too young. But he would always be the baby's father. I told you, we're in love.'

'You're Michael, right?'

'Yeah.'

'What do you think about Yvonne?'

'I love her.'

'You don't just say that to her so that she'll have sex with you?'

'No, I love her. When we first started having sex, I used to say I loved her and I probably didn't mean it. I knew she wouldn't do it unless I said it. But I do love her now.'

'Do you like having sex with her?'

'Yeah, of course I do. Do you think I'm gay?'

'Do you think Yvonne likes it?'

'Yeah. I think she does. She says she does.'
'Does she have orgasms?'
'I don't know. I suppose so. I don't know.'
'She said that sometimes when you have sex you don't use a contraceptive.'
'Yeah. I don't really like using condoms. I mean, I do most of the time 'cause I don't want to get her pregnant. But sometimes I just don't feel like it, or I forget or don't have any.'
'Yvonne doesn't say anything?'
'No.'
'You're not afraid she'll get pregnant?'
'I don't know. I know we should be more careful. But no, I don't really worry about it.'
'What if she got pregnant?'
'I don't know. I don't want a baby. I know Yvonne wouldn't get an abortion. She's said so. I don't know what I'd do.'
'Would you get married?'
'No. I don't know. I don't want to get married. I'm too young. I don't really think about it.'

Michael and Yvonne are perhaps not a typical teenage couple. They are more sexually active than most and perhaps less mature. But there are many adolescents who are as sexually active and who are no more mature in their thinking about what they are doing. Britain still has the highest rate of teenage pregnancy in Western

Europe, in spite of considerable political anxiety about, and attention to, this issue in recent years. In 2005 almost 40,000 girls under the age of eighteen became pregnant and just under 7,500 of those conceptions involved girls under 16. These figures are proving very difficult to shift and in 2004 there were still nearly 350 girls aged only 14 who became pregnant.

The new age of sex

The new teenager does have sex earlier. Not only are teenagers having sex, but they do not see a problem with it. While many worry about pregnancy, sexually transmitted diseases, and parental disapproval, the majority of teenagers simply do not consider it wrong for people their age to have sex.

The same cultural changes that have produced the more outspoken teenager have inaugurated a major change in attitudes about sex. People talk about sex much more openly. Sex between single men and women is not only widely accepted but is done with a casualness that was unthinkable forty years ago. Teenagers are just part of the trend: they have sex earlier, and more casually as well. According to a number of surveys, the average age for first sex is now 16, which is also the legal age of consent. However, the evidence also shows that almost a third of teenagers do not wait that long and have sex before they are 16.

From all that teenagers say about it, they definitely

now feel that sex is a normal part of their lives, and that they have a right to have it – if they so choose. This represents a big change in social norms.

There has especially been a change for girls. Historically there was a big divergence in the numbers of boys and girls having sex under the age of consent. This gap has now almost disappeared, although there is still evidence that girls are more likely to regret their first sexual experience and report being the less willing partner. So whilst the popular perception is that there are plenty of 'ladettes' around, they may in fact not be that happy about what they are doing. Nevertheless, sexual activities that would have previously branded a girl a 'slut' are now okay in the eyes of her peers. The social pressures against sex for girls have dropped sharply.

The increase in working mothers has also had an indirect effect upon teenage sexual activity. As the number of two-parent working families has grown, this has given teenagers more unsupervised time at home. The net result is that teenagers are more sexually active earlier than in prior generations.

Should teenagers have sex?
Should teenagers have sex? Is it bad that they do it so young? In some ways these are not useful questions because they are beside the point. Parents know many reasons why sex isn't a good idea for their teenage children. Many believe deeply that teenage sex is just

simply wrong. But teenagers have sex anyway, and many have no discernible problems in their lives because of it. Some even have a good time.

> *I don't know what your problem is. Me and my boyfriend have been having sex for a year. We do it a lot. We're very careful about protection. I like it. He doesn't take advantage of me. We love each other, but we're probably not going to get married. Neither of us wants to get married until we're a lot older. But we have a real nice time having sex. Not only that, I think my relationship with him is more mature than with anybody else in my life. And the sex is part of it. To tell you the truth, I feel better about myself now than I think I ever did before. And I think I understand more about what a relationship is. I feel now like I'm going to do better later on when I get into other serious relationships, or even when I get married. If you don't like my having sex, that's your problem. It certainly isn't mine.*

Maybe there really are some teenagers for whom having sex is thoroughly enjoyable and for whom it is a wholly positive experience in their lives. But this is an idea parents have a hard time coming to terms with.

Problems of teenage sex

Problems do come up when teenagers have sex. Preg-

239

nancy and sexually transmitted diseases, obviously, but also a subtle emotional problem.

Sex and intimacy

To have sex with somebody is a very intimate experience. Sex carries with it great emotional power. This is true enough for adults. With teenagers, sex, in and of itself, can cause them to 'fall in love'. Perhaps surprisingly, the more seriously broken-hearted teenagers often tend to be boys. After their fairly long sexual relationships have broken up, these boys become very upset and cannot pull themselves out of it. They are less likely than girls to be able to confide in others about their misery. Some have serious thoughts of suicide, though obviously girls too can suffer from such break-ups. There is no question that sex itself can create emotional involvements that are beyond the emotional capacity of the participants. Of course, this is true with some adults too.

And then there's the converse, which really is not much better, particularly with boys. They will engage in sex but are not even close to possessing any real empathy for the girls concerned. And so they must feign caring about the girl and they are aware of the deception. Clearly, this syndrome breeds callousness. These teenagers are unable to combine sex and emotional intimacy because they are too immature to sustain the intimacy. So they end up exploiting their sexual partners; they cannot do otherwise. This sets up a bad pattern for relationships with women in the future.

Gay and lesbian teenagers

'Mum and Dad, there's something I need to talk to you about. It has to do with me.'

' I'm not sure we want to hear this.'

'Now I am a teenager I can no longer deny it. The signs are too clear.'

'You don't need to tell us if you don't want to.'

'Mum and Dad, I am a werewolf.'

'Thank God for that. We thought you were going to tell us you were gay.'

There has been a change over the past generation. Many more gay people have come out. Homosexual activity for both sexes is now legal from the age of 16 and is discussed more openly. Most adults know or are related to someone who is gay or lesbian and there are overtly gay characters on TV, in books and films.

It is certainly far easier to be a gay adult than it was a generation ago. But for gay or lesbian teenagers there has been far less of a change. Non-gay teenagers, especially boys, remain for the most part very intolerant and uncomfortable with gay peers and they regularly use 'gay' as a term of abuse or insult, as in 'Don't be so gay' or 'That is such a gay outfit.'

For most gays the teenage years are the toughest. In

the majority of cases they have a secret about themselves, something that they wish were not true. It is a secret that they correctly perceive would make them immediately vulnerable to ostracism, cruel teasing and possible physical harm. Gay teenagers can feel very lonely and unhappy. It is not surprising that gay teenagers are greater suicide risks than their straight peers.

One change that has made things easier for gay and lesbian teenagers is the Internet. Previously the vast majority of homosexual teenagers lived their homosexuality in isolation from other similarly inclined peers. But now through the Internet they have access to a whole network of others their age, which means they are less isolated.

Yet the immediate world which a gay or lesbian teenager confronts is not so different from the past. A few will come out whilst still at school. If they are lucky enough to live within a tolerant environment they will encounter few problems. Yet most will maintain an apparently 'straight' façade because they are unwilling to stand out and risk the teasing and bullying. It is also common for gay and lesbian teenagers not to reveal their sexuality to their parents. Adolescence is all about separating from parents. Even those matters that previously would have been shared with parents, teenagers choose to keep quiet. And nothing is more private to a teenager than their new sexuality, their sexual feelings.

'How was school today, David?'
'Cool. I got an A in my French test and I got a real
hard-on in History from looking at Sophie Lewis. It
didn't go away until Maths.'
'That's nice, dear.'

If it is anathema for teenagers that their parents might know of their sexual feelings, then how much more so when these feelings are about attraction towards someone of the same sex.

'How was your day at school today, Judy?'
'Not so great. I got C in my French test and I keep
finding it hard to concentrate in History because I have
these continual fantasies about Sophie Lewis who sits
just in front of me, but always acts as if I don't exist.'

Almost invariably during their teenage years most gay and lesbian teenagers will not reveal their sexual preferences to their parents. So how can parents support their possibly gay or lesbian child?

'You don't have to tell us, but we just wanted you to
know that we will love you just as much and will be
just as receptive to you if you are gay. Not that we
think you necessarily are.'
'Mum! Are you crazy? Do you honestly think I am
gay?'

Though well intentioned, such remarks by parents are not particularly helpful. Gay or lesbian children will reveal their sexuality only when they feel comfortable in doing so. More than anything, your children will probably be influenced by what they have observed over the years about your own attitudes towards homosexuality and gay people – whether it is accepting, critical or apparently tolerant, but combined with subtle digs or ridicule.

What can parents do? Try to show a tolerant attitude towards being gay. Be aware of what you say. Every passing comment by parents that denigrates gays is heard by the hypersensitive gay teenager, who concludes 'I couldn't possibly tell my parents' and is thereby cut off from any chance for that support.

Sex in the time of AIDS

AIDS has dramatically changed the potential consequences of sexual activity in both the heterosexual and homosexual communities. Sex with anybody who has had other sexual partners besides oneself carries with it, for the first time since the discovery of penicillin, the risk of contracting what is still potentially a deadly disease.

So far the AIDS epidemic has not hit the teenage population to nearly the extent that it has hit older age groups. But since AIDS' symptoms usually take a number of years to show up in the infected, it is possible that AIDS has spread into the teenage population without yet being apparent. The risk for teenagers is definitely there, and many teenagers are more wary of multiple sexual contacts, or of having sex at all, but the effect of AIDS on their sexual behaviour overall is unclear.

Besides AIDS, there are other less dramatic, but still unpleasant, health effects of unprotected sex. Over the past few years there has been a sharp rise in the number of diagnoses of genital chlamydial infection, genital warts and gonorrhoea. The rise continues to be the steepest in the 16–19 age group. In the decade 1995–2005 there was a threefold increase in the incidence of chlamydia amongst teenage girls, and in just one year from 2004–5 there was a 5 per cent rise in the number of reported cases. This is a particularly insidious disease as it is initially without symptoms, but if left untreated it leads ultimately to infertility. According to present rates of infection, within ten years one in five of all women between 16 and 24 will be infected with chlamydia and a proportion of those will be thereby rendered infertile. According to the Health Protection Agency, diagnoses of herpes rose by 13 per cent and those of genital warts rose by 6 per cent just in the period since 2005. The rise in the use of the pill among young women and the consequent decline in barrier methods of contraception have exacerbated the problems of sexually transmitted diseases in all their forms.

The risk for teenagers is definitely there, and many teenagers are more wary of multiple sexual contacts, or of having sex at all, but the effect of STDs on their sexual behaviour overall is unclear. What is certain is that there continues to be an absolute need for AIDS education for teenagers as well as very clear information about all of the other sexually transmitted diseases that are real risks with sexual activity. It is now a fairly well-established fact that the better and more accurate the information that teenagers get about sex, the more responsible, safer and even less frequent is their sexual activity.

What can parents do?

The parents' main role in relation to sex is education, but most of that should have already taken place by the time their children become adolescents. By then children should know about the changes that will take place in their bodies and in the bodies of the opposite sex. They should know about the process of reproduction. They should know about the sex act itself and they should know that it will be pleasurable, not just functional. Children may not even be that interested in all this information prior to adolescence, but they should have it nonetheless. The fewer surprises in store for them in adolescence, the better. Also, once adolescence strikes, parents are less useful as an information source. Teenagers want to hear lots about sex, but not from their parents. That is too uncomfortable.

*'Well, Tom, I think that it's time that you and I had
a little chat about sex.'*
*'Sure, Dad, but I've heard it a million times. Look,
I've got to go.'*

In fact, he probably does not know it all. He would be
interested in more information – but just not from his
father.

One source of sex information available to all
teenagers is friends. Unfortunately, this may be a case of
the blind leading the blind. Most schools provide some
form of sex education, particularly in the light of AIDS.
That information can be rather limited. Parents should
try to ensure that their teenage children do have access
to full and accurate information about sex. Books about
sex written for teenagers can be particularly useful.
Though the teenagers may show nothing but scorn,
such books rarely go unread. Sometimes family doctors
can be asked and will talk to adolescents about issues of
sexuality when parents are unable to. But if parents feel
that there are certain things about sex that they truly
want their children to know, the only way they can be
certain that this information gets to their children is to
tell them themselves.

Much debated is the question of supplying information about contraception to teenagers, or even the
contraceptives themselves. Does talking about contraception give teenagers the tacit approval of the

authorities, including parents? Does supplying them with contraceptives make it more likely they will have sex, with or without those contraceptives?

Even if there was not the risk of AIDS, it is still preferable that teenagers be given information about contraception and easy access to contraceptives. Set against the very worrying figures for teenage and especially young teenage pregnancy in Britain are the impressive statistics from Holland, where the problem has been successfully contained. In Holland, the number of teenage pregnancies is less than a fifth of those in the UK, a figure often quoted. The big difference is that in the Netherlands there is widespread and easy access to contraception and information about contraceptives, alongside a well-established sex education tradition. The provision of information tells teenagers that their parents recognise they cannot control teenage sexual behaviour, and if teenagers are going to have sex, they certainly should use precautions.

In view of AIDS it becomes highly desirable that adolescents should be supplied with certain very explicit information about sex and about contraception. And they must be supplied with easy access to condoms.

AIDS can be transmitted by having sexual relations with another person. Once the AIDS virus gets in a person's body it lies dormant for one to ten years before symptoms begin to appear. Then, usually within a few years, the person dies. There is still no certain cure. Eventually there may be a vaccine against AIDS. Someday there may be a cast-iron cure for AIDS. Meanwhile, AIDS remains a fatal disease which can be spread by sexual contact. For children to contract AIDS because they did not get information that we adults were reluctant to give them is not acceptable.

Beyond education

Many parents may not be satisfied with simply making sure that their teenagers know the basic facts about sex. They may want to convey more than just facts.

Sex outside of marriage is wrong.

You should only have sex once you are in a sustained, loving relationship.

You may be afraid that if you do not have sex with a boy, then he won't go out with you any more.

Do you want a boy who really only wants to go out with you for the sex?

Parents want to protect their children from hurt and disappointment. And usually they prefer that their children, especially their girls, do not have sex at all.

Although we know teenagers do not like to hear from their parents about much of anything, including sex, we are their parents and we have every right to let them know exactly what we think.

Controlling your teenager's sexual behaviour

Parents, of course, often want more than the role of information- and opinion-giver. They want control.

What's wrong with that? Amelia is 15. I don't want her having sex with boys. She's too young. It is illegal. And besides, I think it's wrong.

They can even try to enforce some rules regarding sexual behaviour – or the lack thereof.

I won't let her go out on dates until she is 16.

I won't let her be at home in the afternoons when there is no adult there.

If she does go out, I will keep close track of exactly where she is and who she's with.

To some extent such supervision probably does make a difference. But in today's world teenagers have the freedom and the opportunity to have sex if they really want to, and as well as being regularly evasive, *in extremis* they are not above sneaking out of their house in the middle of the night to get it. Parents delude themselves if they believe otherwise.

11

Drugs and Drinking

From earliest recorded time human beings have known about the countless substances occurring naturally in the environment which, when ingested or injected or smoked or inhaled, can change moods or states of consciousness. In the last few decades scientists have multiplied this number with seemingly countless unnatural substances and bizarre derivatives from natural ones.

Humankind has known about and manufactured all these potions for the simple reason that day-to-day living can be hard. Life can be stressful. It can be anything but fun, and some of the changes that can be induced chemically can be just the opposite – pleasurable indeed. Many substances have the power to remove the effects of stress. Adults consume alcohol, caffeine, tranquillisers, cocaine and various other drugs in great quantities.

Small wonder, then, that adolescents just entering into adulthood, beset with all the anxieties already discussed in this book, seem to have a craving for mind- and mood-altering substances. In addition, teenagers by their nature like to experiment with new things. They do not like the word 'no'. They do not like to listen to the advice of adults.

It is therefore inevitable that many, if not most, teenagers are going to drink or use drugs. And because many, if not all, of these substances are to some degree physiologically or emotionally addictive and potentially harmful, some teenagers will have substance-abuse problems.

The drug scene – two problems

In the broadest sense there are two distinct teenage drug problems, one of them devastating, the other not nearly so catastrophic. The first involves mainly the inner-city poor and two very serious Class A drugs – heroin and, especially, crack (a concentrated, smokable form of cocaine). The second problem involves the rest of the teenage population – many of whom indulge in a variety of drugs but not, for the most part, heroin and crack – and certainly not on a regular basis.

Amongst the poor in the inner cities, the use of crack has become a serious problem. It is a swiftly addictive drug, much more so than the powder form of cocaine. And it has the power, once the addiction is set, to take over a life and so totally dominate it that all else falls away. It also can be a very nasty drug. When not on a high (and these are very brief with crack), addicts are vulnerable to extreme irritability and depression. It is also a horrendous drug for teenagers. Because of the nature of the addiction there can be a great deal of money to be made, very quickly, by those involved in the selling of crack. This leads to an ever-present need to recruit young drug dealers. More often than not, these kids end up as addicts themselves. But set against the strong financial incentives to go into dealing, the prospect of £5 an hour frying burgers or stacking shelves just cannot compete. Young dealers exert strong pressures on their peers to start using crack. The net result of the crack epidemic is that it is destroying the futures of many youngsters.

The crack scourge of certain inner-city housing estates is a problem both in scope and in origin well beyond the range of this book. In many cases it involves children whose families are already themselves problem drug users. The other teenage drug problem (setting aside the issue of alcohol) concerns the use of marijuana, Ecstasy, solvents and, to a much lesser extent, LSD and powder cocaine. There is much drug use in most secondary schools, but, to keep things in proportion, it is not destroying our youth — apart from the concentrated problem of Class A drug addiction mentioned above.

According to Home Office figures, a third of 14-year-olds will have tried some illicit drug, rising to three-fifths by late adolescence. Cannabis is regularly smoked by children as young as 12. Although there was a decline in drug use between 1995 and 1999, nevertheless in a big international survey of teenagers completed in 1999, Britain was found to have the highest rate of illicit drug use in Europe. And alcohol consumption amongst teenagers has continued to rise. Here too Britain is near the top of the league.

Heavy consumption of alcohol, defined as more than five drinks in a row, has become increasingly common amongst both boys and girls. In fact, one major Europe-wide survey of teenage drinking showed that girls were now outstripping boys in the UK. For many teenagers it is a necessary part of their Friday and Saturday night routine, with boys drinking up to a dozen beers and girls consuming alarming numbers of alcopops or vodka shots. And the recent controversial relaxation in licensing hours has no doubt increased this problem. At its extreme this pattern of heavy drinking may eventually lead to a dependence upon alcohol and there has also been a worrying rise in liver disease amongst young people – not much older than their teens. Meanwhile in the short term there are the unpleasant effects of drunkenness and heavy drinking – fights, trouble with the police, imprudent sexual activity, suicide attempts and tragic deaths in car accidents. In recent years doctors have expressed concern that during peak periods up to 70 per cent of all casualty admissions are drink related.

Although teenage drug habits in general are not a problem on the scale of inner-city heroin abuse, here too there are serious concerns. In the past few years there have been a number of teenage deaths as a result of the use of Ecstasy and this figure has been gradually rising. The most famous case was that of the teenager Leah Betts who died at her eighteenth birthday party. Meanwhile around fifty young people die each year from sniffing glue and butane, usually from cigarette lighters. Although fortunately this number seems to be dropping.

Still, for many teenagers, just as for many adults, drugs and alcohol are part of their fun. Most of these teenagers do not have serious drinking or drug problems. Most will continue the substance use into their adult years, and for most it will not dominate their lives. They will be able to handle it. 'Why do they have to drink or use drugs in order to have a good time?' For the same reason many of the rest of us do, and because the alcohol and the drugs are available. Despite a minimum drinking age of 18, access to alcohol for most teenagers is surprisingly easy. There is a brisk market in the manufacture of fake IDs for those teenagers who want to acquire alcohol or drink in clubs and pubs.

*It's never a problem. Guy's older brother James has a
fake ID and he'll always buy for us. Also, there are
two late-night supermarkets where usually they sell to
anybody. And if we're really desperate one of us hangs
around outside the off-licence and asks people going in
if they'll buy for us. Somebody always will. It's just
not a problem.*

Access to drugs, at least to marijuana, usually presents
little problem either. Most secondary school students
know somebody in their school who deals drugs, or
they know somebody who knows somebody. Some
schools have used aggressive measures to keep drugs out
of their premises, and in some cases this has affected
drug availability, and so drug use. But for the most part
the drugs are there. Whether we like it or not, parents
have very little direct control over whether our children
will or will not drink or use drugs.

*I will tell you exactly what I do. I do not drink or do
any drugs during the week – except maybe if there's a
half-day and we go over to somebody's house in the
afternoon and maybe get high on weed. On the
weekends I go out on both Friday and Saturday nights,
if I can. I don't always drink, but if there's a party, I
usually do. If somebody there has weed, sometimes I'll
smoke that. But I don't like weed all that much. I'd
rather drink.*

I know that when I drink or smoke weed nothing bad is going to happen. I know what I'm doing. I admit I do get drunk sometimes, but I would never drive then, and I don't get rowdy or get into fights.

I'm not an alcoholic, unless everybody who drinks is an alcoholic, and I'm certainly not a drug addict. I know kids who maybe do drink too much, but I don't drink anything like they do. And there are a couple of real druggies in our school, and certainly I'm nothing like them.

But my parents would not understand any of this. What they wouldn't understand is that I'm not a wild kid. I drink and sometimes I smoke weed. I do it to have fun, but I know what I'm doing. I'm never in any danger.

You know what I like best? I like to party, hang out with friends, and either drink or smoke some weed. My parents would have to prove to me that I'm different from other kids, that what I'm doing really is a problem. And I don't think they can.

The influence of parents

Teenagers see themselves as experts. They do not accept that their parents might know as much as they do, and they totally deny that their parents might know anything at all about what's best for them in their own teenage lives.

Parents want to give adolescents freedom but also

keep them free from harm. Teenagers also want freedom from harm but it's not such a high priority with them. Teenagers are more willing to take risks. With their adolescent sense of invulnerability they genuinely believe nothing disastrous could happen to them.

'That's right. I'm willing to trust Jennifer. She can make the right decisions about almost everything. But not about drugs, or drinking. I know what they can do. She doesn't. She thinks she knows. She thinks she knows about everything. But I can remember how naive I was at her age. And it genuinely scares me to think of her out there, on her own, dealing with things that can really harm her, and her just not having the sophistication or maturity to protect herself.'

'I knew my mother was going to say that. She thinks that I don't know anything.'

It would seem that adolescents only listen to themselves. Yet parents do have influence on whether or not their children drink or use drugs. However, as with most issues of adolescence, much of that influence was brought to bear prior to the teenage years.

Children who have developed confidence in themselves are more likely to avoid excessive drinking or drug problems. They are less likely to be influenced by their peers and feel that they have to go along with the crowd.

Families with a strong code of ethics (whether based on religion or not) can influence their children's substance use. Children who are raised in strictly religious homes are much less vulnerable to influences outside the family, and can have much lower substance use. Examples of this phenomenon would be traditional Asian families (either Hindu or Muslim), Orthodox Jews, Evangelical Christians or any group of recently arrived immigrants who live together in closely knit communities in their new country, with a strong sense of family bonds.

But even in families whose day-to-day life is not guided by the rules of a particular faith there can be other kinds of faith and ethics that can make a difference. People often speak of 'family values' or 'moral standards' as buzzwords for what we used to have in our society in the 'good old days' but do not have any more. Obviously this is a very vague and fuzzy area but there is no question that some teenagers have, while others do not, a sense that there is more to their life than the strictly day-to-day. Perhaps this quality could best be described as a sense of purpose.

Maybe this purpose is simply to be successful, to make a lot of money. Maybe it is to excel at sports or in academic subjects or maybe at both. Maybe the purpose is simply to try to do well in one's life, to be a good person. Every human being probably has a purpose in life different from that of everyone else, and as long as these are positive purposes of the kind just identified they can provide a teenager with the idea that life must be more than simply feeling as 'good' as you can all the time. Of course there is the argument that the hallucinogen LSD has sometimes been used in a quest for meaning and for experiencing life as fully as possible – it has even been used by quite genuinely spiritual, if misguided, young people as part of this quest. Centuries ago some of the greatest Romantic poets indulged in similar drugs.

But most drug use cannot claim these high aspirations. Most are of the 'feel-good' variety. Feeling good, or at least okay, is certainly an important part of one's life, but life should be more than that. Those adolescents who understand this, and internalise it, will place less importance on their alcohol and drug use. They can say yes or no without much problem either way. There is no question that teenagers who feel more of an overall purpose and direction in their lives are much less vulnerable to drug abuse than their peers who are less focused. And certainly many such adolescents obtained this sense of purpose mainly from their life at home, inculcated in hundreds of different ways during the course of childhood.

You don't want to be like us, poor, always worrying about money.

You have talent, Jack, you have a chance to be really good.

But even where parents do not point their children towards specific goals, children can internalise a sense that there is more to life than fun right now. Parents who are themselves guided in their day-to-day lives by solid principles (not necessarily formally religious ones) or priorities communicate this 'discipline' almost automatically to their children.

It is self-evident that in the case of drugs, parents need to show by example. If they regularly get drunk, drive after several drinks, smoke heavily or use cannabis then they will have a difficult job persuading their teenagers not to do the same. Whether parents like it or not, what they preach to their children is of little influence compared to what they themselves are like and how they act towards their children. Lectures to adolescents about drug abuse come too late in the day. Much more important is the parental influence all through childhood that has produced, or failed to produce, a sense of purpose in the adolescent. That said, there still remains an important role for parents in resolving their teenager's problems with alcohol and drugs.

What should parents do?

First, parents must decide where they stand. Are they absolutely against any under age drinking or drug use? Many parents, rightly or wrongly, do not mind if their children, especially their sons, drink. Many seem to have a double standard about daughters and drinking. It is interesting that the figures across Europe show greater incidence of drug and drink use amongst boys – although in the UK alcohol consumption by girls has now caught up with and often outstrips that of boys in the most recent surveys. Girls are also more inclined to smoke cigarettes than boys in most European countries. Some parents genuinely do not mind if their children occasionally smoke marijuana, and the downgrading of the classification of cannabis in recent years has encouraged this attitude. Parents must decide where they want to draw the line. That line should not necessarily be drawn at what they find is distasteful, but at what they are willing to live with. The critical line has to be between what they are prepared to put up with on pragmatic grounds and what they absolutely do not want – where they feel their children would be at serious risk. Drawing the line does not give explicit permission for anything less, but rather declares that anything more is out of bounds and dangerous.

Once parents have decided where they stand, what can they do? One possibility is to attempt enforcement. With increased surveillance parents can try to make sure their views on substance use are actually enforced. For example, increased parental surveillance can make it harder for teenagers to get access to and to use alcohol and drugs. There is also a range of drug-testing kits marketed for use in the home. However, total supervision is impossible and parents' ability to control their teenagers' substance use is limited, given the widespread availability of drugs in schools.

Beyond attempted enforcement there remains one other option, and its exercise can have significant influence. Parents can talk to their children. After they decide where they want to draw the line, they should give good and clear reasons for their policy.

> *We do not want you to drink or use any drugs, ever. You may think that you know what you can handle, but you're wrong. Once you start, without your even being aware that it is happening, they can pull you in deeper and deeper. You may think that you can control them, but in the end, they will control you.*

> *We do not want you to smoke marijuana, but we recognise that marijuana is not as dangerous as many other drugs that are out there. Pills of any kind, cocaine, and especially crack, are all very dangerous. Those drugs really scare us. We do not want you to ever use them.*

Their children may not agree with parental policy, but the parents can still hold the line.

> *'Mum, you don't know anything. Ecstasy is no big deal.'*
> *'I think it is, and I think it is very dangerous.'*

*'You're wrong. The worst that can happen is that you
have a bad trip. Some people take it all the time.'*
*'I think it is dangerous and those kids grossly
underestimate its risks, and I do not want you to even
try it. Despite what you may hear, it is dangerous –
not least because you have no idea what a tablet
actually contains. I do not want you to use it.'*

If parents feel strongly about their children drinking or
taking drugs, they should put all their influence on the
line. They should say what they think. This does not
mean that their children will heed their words, but they
may.

Dealing with reality

One cautionary note about talking to teenagers about
drugs or drinking: be wary of preaching a harsher, scarier
anti-substance line than the true dangers warrant. You
risk a credibility gap if you resort to exaggeration.
Teenagers are very fast to turn off adults when they feel
they are being preached at, rather than talked to. If
teenagers feel, rightly or wrongly, that warnings are
being overstated, they will lose trust and will reject the
whole package. If you want to talk to teenagers – a difficult enough task – to begin with you must make sure
that what you say is believable. The best way to ensure
this is to be totally honest. Particularly in regard to drinking and drugs, teenagers do have sources of information

separate from the adult world. This is the 'street wisdom' of their peers, and it's not to be scoffed at. It can be wrong, but at times its information can be more accurate than the adult view. On this as with every other issue of adolescence, if what parents say is too out of line with prevailing teenage wisdom, it is simply not going to be believed. So, for example, dire warnings from a parent about how cannabis will automatically lead on to heroin are not likely to have much impact – especially in an era when even some Conservative Party politicians and senior policemen are calling for the legalisation of marijuana. On the other hand, there is plenty of serious medical opinion that raises concerns about the long-term effects of dope – not least the lung damage associated with any form of smoking – which parents may wish to highlight for their children if they are trying to convince them to keep clear of cannabis.

Drinking and driving

Parental intervention can make a significant difference in regard to drinking and driving. Therefore all parents should address this question directly. No parent should tolerate it. But in order to deliver the message effectively they must get their priorities straight. Parents have only so much influence. They might do well to use it in the cause of not drinking and driving, rather than in lectures about drinking in general:

I don't want you to drink. But above all I don't want
you to come to harm. Please don't drink and drive, and
don't ever get in a car with anyone who does or who
has taken drugs.

This warning should then be repeated throughout their
teenage years.

'Don't worry. I won't drink and drive and I won't be
with anybody who does.'
'I do worry.'

In regard to driving under the influence of drink or
drugs, it is also a good idea to have a special rule about
being stranded:

If you are stranded and the only lift you can get is with
someone who has been drinking, or if you've been
drinking, call us. Call us and we will come and get
you. We will ask no questions. You will not get into
any trouble. Even if calling means that you are caught
in a lie, being in a different place from where you said
you would be or a place you're not supposed to be.
Call us and we will get you. No questions asked.

But if a parent says this, he must really mean it. The rule
sends two excellent messages:

1. The parents place their child's safety over everything else.
2. They feel drinking and driving is so dangerous that they are ready to abandon all other considerations to avoid it.

Some teenagers will still drink and drive. So do many adults, even though attitudes to drink-driving have changed over the past twenty years. But it is important that you communicate your feeling that drinking and driving is in a special category of dangerousness – all in all, the most dangerous threat to the safety of the teenager in general. Here parents can make a difference.

It's against the law

Another source of possible intervention is already in place, and parents don't have to do a thing. Under-age drinking is illegal. Public drunkenness is illegal. Driving while intoxicated is illegal. Drug use is illegal. In recent years Tony Blair's, Jack Straw's and even Prince Charles's teenage sons have been very public examples of how society views drunkenness and drug use.

Get caught by the police using drugs or drinking to excess and you may be prosecuted under the law. At the very least you could be picked up by the police. If you choose to drink or use drugs, what you do is not just between you and us. It is also between you and the law. That is out of our control. We can bail you out of jail, but we can't bail you out of a conviction in a courtroom. If you get caught, you will be answerable to them. And there you will have to take your chances.

Substance-abuse problems

What should parents do if they suspect that their child does have a substance-abuse problem? Perhaps the first rule is that if parents, correctly or not, think that their child has a substance-abuse problem, they should not ignore it. They need to confront their child.

'Doug, I think you have a drug problem. I think you are high most of the time. I don't think you have control of it. I think that you need help.'
'Fuck you! Get out of my life.'

It doesn't matter how the child responds. The point is that the parents are not ignoring the situation, hoping it will somehow just go away. Parents do not want to make it too easy for their child to continue what he or she is doing.

They should also talk to someone who knows more about these problems than they probably do. Many checklists purport to tell the parent what to look for as indications of substance abuse, and most of it is pretty obvious: sudden and sustained irritability, oversleeping, decline in school attendance and marks, and so on.

Parents should not try to diagnose or deal with a problem all on their own. It is very hard to do. Parents and their children need all the help they can get. Substance-abuse problems can be very difficult to deal with, and such problems can go on over a long period of time. They are serious, not 'just a stage' that can be relied on to fade away as the teenager matures. There are a number of helplines and agencies which parents can turn to.

Sometimes teenagers need hospital treatment. Professionals can assess whether this is necessary and they can help to find a suitable clinic.

Of course, any plan of treatment ultimately requires the teenager's active and willing participation. Some can be forced to accept treatment programmes, usually after they have tangled with the law, but none will change unless they buy into the treatment. What happens when a teenager with a substance-abuse problem absolutely refuses to do anything about it? His parents are faced with a very difficult decision about whether to allow their child to live at home. Some do and some do not. When the teenager's problem is destroying the home (literally as well as emotionally, in some cases, because he or she may steal everything of value), parents must look to their own survival. Sometimes all that parents can do is to try to make sure that their own lives are not also destroyed.

12

Suicide

Before talking about teenage suicide it is useful to first look at the statistics on suicide for all ages. They are somewhat surprising, and tell us a lot about the nature of suicide itself.

1. Approximately three times as many men will kill themselves as women. With teenagers this gender ratio is closer to four to one.
2. The suicide rate for teenagers is less than the suicide rate for adults.
3. Suicide by pre-adolescent children is extremely rare.
4. The overall suicide rate has not increased by much. However, that masks the fact that the rate for women has dropped substantially and that for men has increased.

5. The teenage suicide rate, although still lower than for adults (for men it continues to rise in the middle years), has multiplied by two and a half times over the last thirty years, while the overall suicide rate has changed very little.

Why has there been such an increase in teenage suicide? One possibility is that teenagers today face the full range of 'adult' problems at earlier ages than they used to. In a more complicated world with, in many cases, less family support, teenagers feel themselves to be more on their own. This is nobody's 'fault'. It is a different world. Drugs are another reason. Substance abuse increases the likelihood of suicide by lowering inhibitions. The Samaritans report that a third of all young suicides are intoxicated with alcohol at the time of death and a substantial number have taken drugs.

Perhaps of all suicide statistics, the most significant one is the one most taken for granted. It points clearly, if indirectly, to the nature of adolescence: prior to adolescence, with the rarest exception, children do not kill themselves. The idea and the actuality of killing oneself starts only in adolescence. Why?

When a child is absolutely miserable, no matter how miserable he is, he can still look to adults for solace. No matter what the source of misery, children always see nurturing as a possible solution. But with the adolescent mandate, the absolute turning away from just that kind of nurturing, means that this solution is no longer possible. Adolescents are on their own. And now, for the first time in their lives, misery and terrible situations can appear to have no solution.

> 'When I was a young child, I suppose I always knew that if things were really bad, I could go and cry in my mother's arms. But I can't do that now.'
> 'Why not?'
> 'I just can't.'
> 'Even if you felt so bad that you wanted to kill yourself?'
> 'I just can't. It's not there any more.'

Boys compared with girls

Why do four times as many adolescent boys as girls kill themselves? The main reason is probably rather simple, and rather grim. It is the choice of method. Girls attempting suicide will most often take an overdose of pills. Probably the second most common method is wrist cutting. Both of these methods are usually not fatal. Boys also use these methods but they are more likely to employ more lethal means. Boys will shoot themselves, hang themselves, or try to poison themselves with carbon monoxide (car exhaust). Unfortunately, these methods very often work.

Another and very different kind of reason may also partly account for this difference. Since, as we have seen, teenage boys tend to isolate themselves from their parents, they feel they have to keep their problems to themselves. They must work things out on their own. If they cannot, they have few remaining options. Girls, because they at least keep some kind of contact with their parents, do have them to lean on in the worst times.

Substance abuse increases the likelihood of suicide – boys are more likely to drink and take drugs, thereby losing inhibitions, than girls.

Suicide attempts

Many more teenagers try to kill themselves than succeed. Statistics on attempts are not very reliable, but girls probably make more attempts than boys. Each year around 24,000 15–19-year-olds are admitted to hospital as a result of deliberately self-harming themselves. (Although a great many more episodes of self-harm do not result in a hospital visit.) And girls are four times as likely to indulge in such behaviour as boys.

When a teenager attempts to kill himself or herself and does not succeed, did he or she really want to end their lives or was their action a cry for help, or merely a misguided way of getting attention? Did they really want to die? Who knows? Did the teenagers who succeeded in killing themselves really want to die? A suicide attempt is desperate regardless of what was behind it. All suicide attempts are serious.

Why do teenagers try to kill themselves?

Teenagers try to kill themselves for pretty much the same reasons as adults. They may have been very depressed for a long time. They may have been rejected by a lover or face sustained bullying at school. They may feel under such pressure that they simply 'can't go on any more'. Social isolation. Unemployment. There are many reasons. But there is at least one characteristic of many teenage suicide attempts that is different from those of adults. More suicide attempts by teenagers are 'spur of the moment', in reaction to a specific and immediate situation to which they see no solution.

Depression and suicide

Teenagers can also suffer from serious depression. Depression in this sense means an ongoing condition wherein a teenager feels 'down', unhappy, has difficulty in generating enthusiasm about anything at all, lacks energy. Depression may be in reaction to a specific situation – for example, a parent's death – or it may not seem to stem from any particular external cause. Some depressions are now believed to have mainly biochemical causes. In addition, depression can be a concomitant of drug or alcohol abuse.

Depression over a sustained period of time, from whatever cause, can lead to suicide attempts. Teenagers in these situations often respond to counselling, and sometimes to anti-depressant medication. But many have emotional conditions that stay with them through and beyond adolescence. Their suicide attempts may not end with adolescence.

They can't see tomorrow

The following are some reasons why teenagers have tried to kill themselves:

1. In a rage after a big fight with parents that started over something trivial, a household chore left undone, perhaps.
2. After a break-up with a girlfriend or boyfriend (probably the single most frequent cause of teenage suicide attempts).
3. After receiving a bad school report, when parents had said this report had better be an improvement 'or else'.
4. When school is about to re-start after the summer or Christmas holiday (the anxiety for some can be overwhelming).
5. After getting in trouble for crashing the car (and not necessarily seriously), being arrested (again, perhaps on a minor charge).
6. When unable to decide whether they should live with their father or mother after a divorce (as an adolescent, it will be their decision if both parents want them).

Common to all these situations is the particular teenage phenomenon discussed earlier, the conviction that there is no tomorrow. Teenagers can feel trapped in situations to which they see no solution, and from which they see no escape. They look at tomorrow and it seems just too awful. These suicide attempts are a teenager's lack of perspective taken to its limits. In many cases all they have to do is wait a little while. But this they do not yet know.

Intervention

It is encouraging news that adult intervention can make a big difference in potential teenage suicide because in this case teenagers are often prepared to hand over the responsibility for their problems to someone else, at least temporarily. Involvement by almost any adult lets a teenager exit safely from a situation they feel they cannot deal with. They may have to deal with it later, but the crisis is relieved for now.

With potentially suicidal teenagers, friends can be significantly less useful than adults. Yet not infrequently friends find themselves saddled with a terrible secret.

Please, Kirsty, you have to swear to God that you won't tell anybody how I feel. I'm just telling you because you're my best friend and I need somebody to talk to.

Yet the Kirstys of the world are often not enough help. They do not have enough of a perspective either. The burden for them is too great. It is always preferable for teenagers to tell some adult if they know a friend is having very serious problems, even if, as in Kirsty's case here, she would be betraying a promise. The burden of keeping a friend alive is an awfully big burden. The adult world really can do a better job.

What to do
If a parent has any worry at all that her child may be thinking about killing himself or herself, she should ask directly.

Roger, do you think about killing yourself?

Parents are often very reluctant to ask such a question because they fear that in asking they may somehow create a possibility that did not exist before. They fear the question may put the idea into their child's head: 'I wasn't until now. But now that you bring it up, Mum, it seems like a very good idea.'

'Can you promise me that if I ask him about suicide, the question won't put the idea in his head? Can you promise me that he will not, later on, try to kill himself?' There are never guarantees, but certainly the risks of not asking a troubled teenager are far greater than the risks of asking. The teenager may be lying when denying the thought, but at least you have asked. At least he knows that you know something is wrong. He knows the line of communication is always open.

Well, I just wanted to ask, because I worry. But if you ever do think about killing yourself, or harming yourself, before you do anything, talk to me or your father first. Okay?

If they say 'yes'
Yeah, sometimes.

If adolescents admit to thinking about killing themselves, this is not necessarily a disaster. Many do. But the admission should always be taken seriously. The first point to determine is if there is an immediate danger. If the child admits he is seriously thinking about suicide in the near future, it is time to get immediate help. This means calling the family doctor, or a mental health professional if the parents know one. The best course might be calling a helpline such as the Samaritans. Parents need to talk to someone experienced in dealing with potentially suicidal teenagers. Often it may be useful to get the child to talk to a professional as soon as possible to determine whether immediate medical attention or admission to hospital is necessary. If not, do the parents need to keep a twenty-four-hour watch on their child?

These are steps that rarely need to be taken. But just

knowing that one is ready to take these steps, if necessary, can make the issue of suicide less, not more, scary. The goal with any teenager who does talk about the possibility of suicide is to get him into counselling, even if the situation is not critical. Good counselling really can make a difference when teenagers are in trouble.

Warning signs

As discussed, teenagers may try to kill themselves for many different reasons. But where is the line between non-suicidal misery and potentially suicidal misery? How can a parent tell? Beyond certain very definite warning signs it is not possible to be certain. Adolescence is often an unhappy experience. Being thoroughly miserable is not uncommon with normal teenagers, and this can be for all sorts of obscure and highly personal reasons. When should parents start to be concerned? Probably the best answer is when the misery continues; when a teenager does not seem to have ups and downs, but mainly just downs, and when this pattern continues, not for a week or two, but for many weeks, a month, two months.

This is when parents might do well to consult a mental health professional who has experience with teenagers. This professional will want to talk in depth to the teenager. Afterwards the parents can then ask: Should we be worried? Is there anything we can do to help? Would it be helpful if our child had regular counselling?

The vital warning sign

The one warning sign that must not be ignored is when teenagers talk about wanting to die. Not all such talk means that a teenager is contemplating suicide, but most teenagers who do try to kill themselves talk about it first, perhaps in a letter left lying around, or in a school essay reported to parents by a concerned teacher, or simply in things said at home.

I don't know. Life really is shit. What's the point?

You and Dad care so much about my results. If I do really badly this term, maybe I'll just kill myself, then I won't have to worry about it any more.

Maybe everybody would be happier if I just wasn't here any more.

Such remarks should not be ignored. Parents should ask directly whether the teenager really feels like killing himself. As discussed earlier, depending on the response, appropriate steps should be taken. There are no guarantees, but if parents are aware of their children and willing to be a bit intrusive when they believe it's warranted, they can head off many potential tragedies.

'You're sure you don't want to kill yourself?'
'No, Mum. Please. I promise. I'm really not going to.'

CONCLUSION

The End of Adolescence

'Is this really you, Max?'

'What do you mean, Mum? Why?'

'But you're being so nice.'

'Yeah. What's so strange about that?'

*'But it's been so long since you've been nice. Do you
see what you are doing right now?'*

*'Yeah, I'm helping you clear the supper table. What's
the big deal?'*

*'But at the end of the meal you just got up and started
clearing away the plates. I didn't ask you to do it, or
anything. And you've been very pleasant about it, as if
you really want to help me.'*

'Yeah, well, I do. You made the meal, and you have

had a busy day.'
'Wow — you haven't said anything like that since you
were 11. All these years, this is exactly how I wanted
you to act, and now, suddenly, you're doing it. I don't
understand.'
'I don't know. I guess I was kind of a prat. But now
I'm older. I'm not a kid any more. I know how hard
you and Dad work.'

Max's mother blinks away the tears.

'Hello, Joanna.'
'Hi, Dad. How was work?'
'What?'
'How was work? Anything special happen today? You
know, any interesting clients or anything?'
'What?'
'Why do you keep saying "What"?'

For, again, they have changed. And almost always the
change is for the better, and often enormously for the
better. They are friendly. Co-operative. Civilised. Willing to take out the rubbish. The girls no longer disagree
with everything you say, nor do they criticise you constantly. The boys talk pleasantly and even, if that is their
nature, a lot. Moreover, they genuinely seem to like
you. They show it, they might even say it — with no
embarrassment.

Not all teenagers change in this way, but most do. What's going on? Time. Mainly just time. Nature has spoken at last. The needs of the baby self are no longer so great. They are genuinely able to behave in a more responsible, less self-centred manner. The more mature version of the self that for years had been on display only away from home can now be seen in the kitchen as well, at least some of the time.

The adolescent mandate to strive for independence has finally achieved its goal. The teenagers are on their own and they seem to be able to survive. They are independent. They really do not need their parents any more. Their parents are no longer a threat. It is possible to have warm feelings towards them, to care about them, because these feelings are no longer a challenge to their sense of independence. The sexuality of adolescent boys, previously unfocused and all over the place, is now satisfactorily under control, focused quite keenly on favourite partners outside the home, clearing the way for affectionate feelings towards the mother that will not be sexually tinged. They are pleasant. They like you. They can be in the same room as you.

Remember: it's a stage

It is very important for parents to understand that adolescence does have an end, that teenagers do change. When parents are going through their children's adolescence they need to know they are witnessing a stage.

Granted, some children continue right through their adult lives being irresponsible, self-centred, needing always to be nurtured, never truly establishing their own independence. But parents can be fairly certain that most children will change automatically, and for the better. This knowledge can make the bad parts seem not quite so desperate. Even the immature teenagers who turn out to be a continuing burden to their parents tend to grow more pleasant in their demands. The unabated nastiness does run its course and fade away.

I hate you and I hate Daddy and I'm not going back to school, and I don't care what you do to me.

'You're sure that she's going to change? You promise me? Is there really light at the end of this tunnel?' Ultimately, much of being the parent of a teenager is a matter of faith – that adolescence is a stage, particularly the adolescence of one's own child. Dealing with the new teenager can be pretty rough. At such times it is necessary to know that, awful as they may seem, the end product is going to be so much better.

Yet this is so. Not only that, but of all the parental interventions, admonitions and advice that seem so fruitlessly to bounce off one's child, some do get through. Parents' efforts during the teenage years not only do have an impact; they are often crucial. Only sometimes this is not always so easy to see!